C-837 CAREER EXAMINATION SERIES

***This is your PASSBOOK for...***

# Correction Officer I

***Test Preparation Study Guide***
***Questions & Answers***

NLC®
NATIONAL LEARNING CORPORATION®

# COPYRIGHT NOTICE



**National Learning Corporation**

212 Michael Drive, Syosset, NY 11791
(516) 921-8888 • www.passbooks.com
E-mail: info@passbooks.com

PUBLISHED IN THE UNITED STATES OF AMERICA

# PASSBOOK® SERIES

THE *PASSBOOK® SERIES* has been created to prepare applicants and candidates for the ultimate academic battlefield – the examination room.

At some time in our lives, each and every one of us may be required to take an examination – for validation, matriculation, admission, qualification, registration, certification, or licensure.

Based on the assumption that every applicant or candidate has met the basic formal educational standards, has taken the required number of courses, and read the necessary texts, the *PASSBOOK® SERIES* furnishes the one special preparation which may assure passing with confidence, instead of failing with insecurity. Examination questions – together with answers – are furnished as the basic vehicle for study so that the mysteries of the examination and its compounding difficulties may be eliminated or diminished by a sure method.

This book is meant to help you pass your examination provided that you qualify and are serious in your objective.

The entire field is reviewed through the huge store of content information which is succinctly presented through a provocative and challenging approach – the question-and-answer method.

A climate of success is established by furnishing the correct answers at the end of each test.

You soon learn to recognize types of questions, forms of questions, and patterns of questioning. You may even begin to anticipate expected outcomes.

You perceive that many questions are repeated or adapted so that you can gain acute insights, which may enable you to score many sure points.

You learn how to confront new questions, or types of questions, and to attack them confidently and work out the correct answers.

You note objectives and emphases, and recognize pitfalls and dangers, so that you may make positive educational adjustments.

Moreover, you are kept fully informed in relation to new concepts, methods, practices, and directions in the field.

You discover that you are actually taking the examination all the time: you are preparing for the examination by "taking" an examination, not by reading extraneous and/or supererogatory textbooks.

In short, this PASSBOOK®, used directedly, should be an important factor in helping you to pass your test.

# CORRECTION OFFICER I

## DUTIES

Guards prisoners and maintains order and security at the county detention and correctional facilities. Advises inmates of the rules and regulations governing the operation of the facility. Supervises the daily living activities of inmates including eating, cleaning and assigned duties. Conducts searches of prisoners and calls for contraband. May be required to carry firearms in the performance of certain duties. Does related work as required.

## SCOPE OF THE EXAMINATION

The written test will cover knowledge, skills, and/or abilities in such areas as:

1. Understanding and applying rules and regulations related to the security and control of correctional inmates;
2. Understanding and interpreting written material; and
3. Preparing written material.

# HOW TO TAKE A TEST

## I. YOU MUST PASS AN EXAMINATION

### *A. WHAT EVERY CANDIDATE SHOULD KNOW*

Examination applicants often ask us for help in preparing for the written test. What can I study in advance? What kinds of questions will be asked? How will the test be given? How will the papers be graded?

As an applicant for a civil service examination, you may be wondering about some of these things. Our purpose here is to suggest effective methods of advance study and to describe civil service examinations.

Your chances for success on this examination can be increased if you know how to prepare. Those "pre-examination jitters" can be reduced if you know what to expect. You can even experience an adventure in good citizenship if you know why civil service exams are given.

### *B. WHY ARE CIVIL SERVICE EXAMINATIONS GIVEN?*

Civil service examinations are important to you in two ways. As a citizen, you want public jobs filled by employees who know how to do their work. As a job seeker, you want a fair chance to compete for that job on an equal footing with other candidates. The best-known means of accomplishing this two-fold goal is the competitive examination.

Exams are widely publicized throughout the nation. They may be administered for jobs in federal, state, city, municipal, town or village governments or agencies.

Any citizen may apply, with some limitations, such as the age or residence of applicants. Your experience and education may be reviewed to see whether you meet the requirements for the particular examination. When these requirements exist, they are reasonable and applied consistently to all applicants. Thus, a competitive examination may cause you some uneasiness now, but it is your privilege and safeguard.

### *C. HOW ARE CIVIL SERVICE EXAMS DEVELOPED?*

Examinations are carefully written by trained technicians who are specialists in the field known as "psychological measurement," in consultation with recognized authorities in the field of work that the test will cover. These experts recommend the subject matter areas or skills to be tested; only those knowledges or skills important to your success on the job are included. The most reliable books and source materials available are used as references. Together, the experts and technicians judge the difficulty level of the questions.

Test technicians know how to phrase questions so that the problem is clearly stated. Their ethics do not permit "trick" or "catch" questions. Questions may have been tried out on sample groups, or subjected to statistical analysis, to determine their usefulness.

Written tests are often used in combination with performance tests, ratings of training and experience, and oral interviews. All of these measures combine to form the best-known means of finding the right person for the right job.

## II. HOW TO PASS THE WRITTEN TEST

### *A. NATURE OF THE EXAMINATION*

To prepare intelligently for civil service examinations, you should know how they differ from school examinations you have taken. In school you were assigned certain definite pages to read or subjects to cover. The examination questions were quite detailed and usually emphasized memory. Civil service exams, on the other hand, try to discover your present ability to perform the duties of a position, plus your potentiality to learn these duties. In other words, a civil service exam attempts to predict how successful you will be. Questions cover such a broad area that they cannot be as minute and detailed as school exam questions.

In the public service similar kinds of work, or positions, are grouped together in one "class." This process is known as *position-classification.* All the positions in a class are paid according to the salary range for that class. One class title covers all of these positions, and they are all tested by the same examination.

### *B. FOUR BASIC STEPS*

#### 1) Study the announcement

How, then, can you know what subjects to study? Our best answer is: "Learn as much as possible about the class of positions for which you've applied." The exam will test the knowledge, skills and abilities needed to do the work.

Your most valuable source of information about the position you want is the official exam announcement. This announcement lists the training and experience qualifications. Check these standards and apply only if you come reasonably close to meeting them.

The brief description of the position in the examination announcement offers some clues to the subjects which will be tested. Think about the job itself. Review the duties in your mind. Can you perform them, or are there some in which you are rusty? Fill in the blank spots in your preparation.

Many jurisdictions preview the written test in the exam announcement by including a section called "Knowledge and Abilities Required," "Scope of the Examination," or some similar heading. Here you will find out specifically what fields will be tested.

#### 2) Review your own background

Once you learn in general what the position is all about, and what you need to know to do the work, ask yourself which subjects you already know fairly well and which need improvement. You may wonder whether to concentrate on improving your strong areas or on building some background in your fields of weakness. When the announcement has specified "some knowledge" or "considerable knowledge," or has used adjectives like "beginning principles of..." or "advanced ... methods," you can get a clue as to the number and difficulty of questions to be asked in any given field. More questions, and hence broader coverage, would be included for those subjects which are more important in the work. Now weigh your strengths and weaknesses against the job requirements and prepare accordingly.

#### 3) Determine the level of the position

Another way to tell how intensively you should prepare is to understand the level of the job for which you are applying. Is it the entering level? In other words, is this the position in which beginners in a field of work are hired? Or is it an intermediate or advanced level? Sometimes this is indicated by such words as "Junior" or "Senior" in the class title. Other jurisdictions use Roman numerals to designate the level – Clerk I, Clerk II, for example. The word "Supervisor" sometimes appears in the title. If the level is not indicated by the title, check the description of duties. Will you be working under very close supervision, or will you have responsibility for independent decisions in this work?

**4) Choose appropriate study materials**

Now that you know the subjects to be examined and the relative amount of each subject to be covered, you can choose suitable study materials. For beginning level jobs, or even advanced ones, if you have a pronounced weakness in some aspect of your training, read a modern, standard textbook in that field. Be sure it is up to date and has general coverage. Such books are normally available at your library, and the librarian will be glad to help you locate one. For entry-level positions, questions of appropriate difficulty are chosen – neither highly advanced questions, nor those too simple. Such questions require careful thought but not advanced training.

If the position for which you are applying is technical or advanced, you will read more advanced, specialized material. If you are already familiar with the basic principles of your field, elementary textbooks would waste your time. Concentrate on advanced textbooks and technical periodicals. Think through the concepts and review difficult problems in your field.

These are all general sources. You can get more ideas on your own initiative, following these leads. For example, training manuals and publications of the government agency which employs workers in your field can be useful, particularly for technical and professional positions. A letter or visit to the government department involved may result in more specific study suggestions, and certainly will provide you with a more definite idea of the exact nature of the position you are seeking.

## III. KINDS OF TESTS

Tests are used for purposes other than measuring knowledge and ability to perform specified duties. For some positions, it is equally important to test ability to make adjustments to new situations or to profit from training. In others, basic mental abilities not dependent on information are essential. Questions which test these things may not appear as pertinent to the duties of the position as those which test for knowledge and information. Yet they are often highly important parts of a fair examination. For very general questions, it is almost impossible to help you direct your study efforts. What we can do is to point out some of the more common of these general abilities needed in public service positions and describe some typical questions.

1) General information

Broad, general information has been found useful for predicting job success in some kinds of work. This is tested in a variety of ways, from vocabulary lists to questions about current events. Basic background in some field of work, such as sociology or economics, may be sampled in a group of questions. Often these are principles which have become familiar to most persons through exposure rather than through formal training. It is difficult to advise you how to study for these questions; being alert to the world around you is our best suggestion.

2) Verbal ability

An example of an ability needed in many positions is verbal or language ability. Verbal ability is, in brief, the ability to use and understand words. Vocabulary and grammar tests are typical measures of this ability. Reading comprehension or paragraph interpretation questions are common in many kinds of civil service tests. You are given a paragraph of written material and asked to find its central meaning.

3) Numerical ability

Number skills can be tested by the familiar arithmetic problem, by checking paired lists of numbers to see which are alike and which are different, or by interpreting charts and graphs. In the latter test, a graph may be printed in the test booklet which you are asked to use as the basis for answering questions.

4) Observation

A popular test for law-enforcement positions is the observation test. A picture is shown to you for several minutes, then taken away. Questions about the picture test your ability to observe both details and larger elements.

5) Following directions

In many positions in the public service, the employee must be able to carry out written instructions dependably and accurately. You may be given a chart with several columns, each column listing a variety of information. The questions require you to carry out directions involving the information given in the chart.

6) Skills and aptitudes

Performance tests effectively measure some manual skills and aptitudes. When the skill is one in which you are trained, such as typing or shorthand, you can practice. These tests are often very much like those given in business school or high school courses. For many of the other skills and aptitudes, however, no short-time preparation can be made. Skills and abilities natural to you or that you have developed throughout your lifetime are being tested.

Many of the general questions just described provide all the data needed to answer the questions and ask you to use your reasoning ability to find the answers. Your best preparation for these tests, as well as for tests of facts and ideas, is to be at your physical and mental best. You, no doubt, have your own methods of getting into an exam-taking mood and keeping "in shape." The next section lists some ideas on this subject.

## IV. KINDS OF QUESTIONS

Only rarely is the "essay" question, which you answer in narrative form, used in civil service tests. Civil service tests are usually of the short-answer type. Full instructions for answering these questions will be given to you at the examination. But in case this is your first experience with short-answer questions and separate answer sheets, here is what you need to know:

**1) Multiple-choice Questions**

Most popular of the short-answer questions is the "multiple choice" or "best answer" question. It can be used, for example, to test for factual knowledge, ability to solve problems or judgment in meeting situations found at work.

A multiple-choice question is normally one of three types—

- It can begin with an incomplete statement followed by several possible endings. You are to find the one ending which *best* completes the statement, although some of the others may not be entirely wrong.
- It can also be a complete statement in the form of a question which is answered by choosing one of the statements listed.

- It can be in the form of a problem – again you select the best answer.

Here is an example of a multiple-choice question with a discussion which should give you some clues as to the method for choosing the right answer:

When an employee has a complaint about his assignment, the action which will *best* help him overcome his difficulty is to

A. discuss his difficulty with his coworkers
B. take the problem to the head of the organization
C. take the problem to the person who gave him the assignment
D. say nothing to anyone about his complaint

In answering this question, you should study each of the choices to find which is best. Consider choice "A" – Certainly an employee may discuss his complaint with fellow employees, but no change or improvement can result, and the complaint remains unresolved. Choice "B" is a poor choice since the head of the organization probably does not know what assignment you have been given, and taking your problem to him is known as "going over the head" of the supervisor. The supervisor, or person who made the assignment, is the person who can clarify it or correct any injustice. Choice "C" is, therefore, correct. To say nothing, as in choice "D," is unwise. Supervisors have and interest in knowing the problems employees are facing, and the employee is seeking a solution to his problem.

**2) True/False Questions**

The "true/false" or "right/wrong" form of question is sometimes used. Here a complete statement is given. Your job is to decide whether the statement is right or wrong.

SAMPLE: A roaming cell-phone call to a nearby city costs less than a non-roaming call to a distant city.

This statement is wrong, or false, since roaming calls are more expensive.

This is not a complete list of all possible question forms, although most of the others are variations of these common types. You will always get complete directions for answering questions. Be sure you understand *how* to mark your answers – ask questions until you do.

## V. RECORDING YOUR ANSWERS

Computer terminals are used more and more today for many different kinds of exams.

For an examination with very few applicants, you may be told to record your answers in the test booklet itself. Separate answer sheets are much more common. If this separate answer sheet is to be scored by machine – and this is often the case – it is highly important that you mark your answers correctly in order to get credit.

An electronic scoring machine is often used in civil service offices because of the speed with which papers can be scored. Machine-scored answer sheets must be marked with a pencil, which will be given to you. This pencil has a high graphite content which responds to the electronic scoring machine. As a matter of fact, stray dots may register as answers, so do not let your pencil rest on the answer sheet while you are pondering the correct answer. Also, if your pencil lead breaks or is otherwise defective, ask for another.

Since the answer sheet will be dropped in a slot in the scoring machine, be careful not to bend the corners or get the paper crumpled.

The answer sheet normally has five vertical columns of numbers, with 30 numbers to a column. These numbers correspond to the question numbers in your test booklet. After each number, going across the page are four or five pairs of dotted lines. These short dotted lines have small letters or numbers above them. The first two pairs may also have a "T" or "F" above the letters. This indicates that the first two pairs only are to be used if the questions are of the true-false type. If the questions are multiple choice, disregard the "T" and "F" and pay attention only to the small letters or numbers.

Answer your questions in the manner of the sample that follows:

32. The largest city in the United States is
    A. Washington, D.C.
    B. New York City
    C. Chicago
    D. Detroit
    E. San Francisco

1) Choose the answer you think is best. (New York City is the largest, so "B" is correct.)
2) Find the row of dotted lines numbered the same as the question you are answering. (Find row number 32)
3) Find the pair of dotted lines corresponding to the answer. (Find the pair of lines under the mark "B.")
4) Make a solid black mark between the dotted lines.

## VI. BEFORE THE TEST

Common sense will help you find procedures to follow to get ready for an examination. Too many of us, however, overlook these sensible measures. Indeed, nervousness and fatigue have been found to be the most serious reasons why applicants fail to do their best on civil service tests. Here is a list of reminders:

- Begin your preparation early – Don't wait until the last minute to go scurrying around for books and materials or to find out what the position is all about.
- Prepare continuously – An hour a night for a week is better than an all-night cram session. This has been definitely established. What is more, a night a week for a month will return better dividends than crowding your study into a shorter period of time.
- Locate the place of the exam – You have been sent a notice telling you when and where to report for the examination. If the location is in a different town or otherwise unfamiliar to you, it would be well to inquire the best route and learn something about the building.
- Relax the night before the test – Allow your mind to rest. Do not study at all that night. Plan some mild recreation or diversion; then go to bed early and get a good night's sleep.
- Get up early enough to make a leisurely trip to the place for the test – This way unforeseen events, traffic snarls, unfamiliar buildings, etc. will not upset you.
- Dress comfortably – A written test is not a fashion show. You will be known by number and not by name, so wear something comfortable.

- Leave excess paraphernalia at home – Shopping bags and odd bundles will get in your way. You need bring only the items mentioned in the official notice you received; usually everything you need is provided. Do not bring reference books to the exam. They will only confuse those last minutes and be taken away from you when in the test room.
- Arrive somewhat ahead of time – If because of transportation schedules you must get there very early, bring a newspaper or magazine to take your mind off yourself while waiting.
- Locate the examination room – When you have found the proper room, you will be directed to the seat or part of the room where you will sit. Sometimes you are given a sheet of instructions to read while you are waiting. Do not fill out any forms until you are told to do so; just read them and be prepared.
- Relax and prepare to listen to the instructions
- If you have any physical problem that may keep you from doing your best, be sure to tell the test administrator. If you are sick or in poor health, you really cannot do your best on the exam. You can come back and take the test some other time.

## VII. AT THE TEST

The day of the test is here and you have the test booklet in your hand. The temptation to get going is very strong. Caution! There is more to success than knowing the right answers. You must know how to identify your papers and understand variations in the type of short-answer question used in this particular examination. Follow these suggestions for maximum results from your efforts:

**1) Cooperate with the monitor**

The test administrator has a duty to create a situation in which you can be as much at ease as possible. He will give instructions, tell you when to begin, check to see that you are marking your answer sheet correctly, and so on. He is not there to guard you, although he will see that your competitors do not take unfair advantage. He wants to help you do your best.

**2) Listen to all instructions**

Don't jump the gun! Wait until you understand all directions. In most civil service tests you get more time than you need to answer the questions. So don't be in a hurry. Read each word of instructions until you clearly understand the meaning. Study the examples, listen to all announcements and follow directions. Ask questions if you do not understand what to do.

**3) Identify your papers**

Civil service exams are usually identified by number only. You will be assigned a number; you must not put your name on your test papers. Be sure to copy your number correctly. Since more than one exam may be given, copy your exact examination title.

**4) Plan your time**

Unless you are told that a test is a "speed" or "rate of work" test, speed itself is usually not important. Time enough to answer all the questions will be provided, but this does not mean that you have all day. An overall time limit has been set. Divide the total time (in minutes) by the number of questions to determine the approximate time you have for each question.

**5) Do not linger over difficult questions**

If you come across a difficult question, mark it with a paper clip (useful to have along) and come back to it when you have been through the booklet. One caution if you do this – be sure to skip a number on your answer sheet as well. Check often to be sure that you have not lost your place and that you are marking in the row numbered the same as the question you are answering.

**6) Read the questions**

Be sure you know what the question asks! Many capable people are unsuccessful because they failed to *read* the questions correctly.

**7) Answer all questions**

Unless you have been instructed that a penalty will be deducted for incorrect answers, it is better to guess than to omit a question.

**8) Speed tests**

It is often better NOT to guess on speed tests. It has been found that on timed tests people are tempted to spend the last few seconds before time is called in marking answers at random – without even reading them – in the hope of picking up a few extra points. To discourage this practice, the instructions may warn you that your score will be "corrected" for guessing. That is, a penalty will be applied. The incorrect answers will be deducted from the correct ones, or some other penalty formula will be used.

**9) Review your answers**

If you finish before time is called, go back to the questions you guessed or omitted to give them further thought. Review other answers if you have time.

**10) Return your test materials**

If you are ready to leave before others have finished or time is called, take ALL your materials to the monitor and leave quietly. Never take any test material with you. The monitor can discover whose papers are not complete, and taking a test booklet may be grounds for disqualification.

## VIII. EXAMINATION TECHNIQUES

1) Read the general instructions carefully. These are usually printed on the first page of the exam booklet. As a rule, these instructions refer to the timing of the examination; the fact that you should not start work until the signal and must stop work at a signal, etc. If there are any *special* instructions, such as a choice of questions to be answered, make sure that you note this instruction carefully.

2) When you are ready to start work on the examination, that is as soon as the signal has been given, read the instructions to each question booklet, underline any key words or phrases, such as *least*, *best*, *outline*, *describe* and the like. In this way you will tend to answer as requested rather than discover on reviewing your paper that you *listed without describing*, that you selected the *worst* choice rather than the *best* choice, etc.

3) If the examination is of the objective or multiple-choice type – that is, each question will also give a series of possible answers: A, B, C or D, and you are called upon to select the best answer and write the letter next to that answer on your answer paper – it is advisable to start answering each question in turn. There may be anywhere from 50 to 100 such questions in the three or four hours allotted and you can see how much time would be taken if you read through all the questions before beginning to answer any. Furthermore, if you come across a question or group of questions which you know would be difficult to answer, it would undoubtedly affect your handling of all the other questions.

4) If the examination is of the essay type and contains but a few questions, it is a moot point as to whether you should read all the questions before starting to answer any one. Of course, if you are given a choice – say five out of seven and the like – then it is essential to read all the questions so you can eliminate the two that are most difficult. If, however, you are asked to answer all the questions, there may be danger in trying to answer the easiest one first because you may find that you will spend too much time on it. The best technique is to answer the first question, then proceed to the second, etc.

5) Time your answers. Before the exam begins, write down the time it started, then add the time allowed for the examination and write down the time it must be completed, then divide the time available somewhat as follows:
   - If 3-1/2 hours are allowed, that would be 210 minutes. If you have 80 objective-type questions, that would be an average of 2-1/2 minutes per question. Allow yourself no more than 2 minutes per question, or a total of 160 minutes, which will permit about 50 minutes to review.
   - If for the time allotment of 210 minutes there are 7 essay questions to answer, that would average about 30 minutes a question. Give yourself only 25 minutes per question so that you have about 35 minutes to review.

6) The most important instruction is to *read each question* and make sure you know what is wanted. The second most important instruction is to *time yourself properly* so that you answer every question. The third most important instruction is to *answer every question.* Guess if you have to but include something for each question. Remember that you will receive no credit for a blank and will probably receive some credit if you write something in answer to an essay question. If you guess a letter – say "B" for a multiple-choice question – you may have guessed right. If you leave a blank as an answer to a multiple-choice question, the examiners may respect your feelings but it will not add a point to your score. Some exams may penalize you for wrong answers, so in such cases *only*, you may not want to guess unless you have some basis for your answer.

7) Suggestions
   a. Objective-type questions
      1. Examine the question booklet for proper sequence of pages and questions
      2. Read all instructions carefully
      3. Skip any question which seems too difficult; return to it after all other questions have been answered
      4. Apportion your time properly; do not spend too much time on any single question or group of questions

5. Note and underline key words – *all, most, fewest, least, best, worst, same, opposite,* etc.
6. Pay particular attention to negatives
7. Note unusual option, e.g., unduly long, short, complex, different or similar in content to the body of the question
8. Observe the use of "hedging" words – *probably, may, most likely,* etc.
9. Make sure that your answer is put next to the same number as the question
10. Do not second-guess unless you have good reason to believe the second answer is definitely more correct
11. Cross out original answer if you decide another answer is more accurate; do not erase until you are ready to hand your paper in
12. Answer all questions; guess unless instructed otherwise
13. Leave time for review

b. Essay questions
1. Read each question carefully
2. Determine exactly what is wanted. Underline key words or phrases.
3. Decide on outline or paragraph answer
4. Include many different points and elements unless asked to develop any one or two points or elements
5. Show impartiality by giving pros and cons unless directed to select one side only
6. Make and write down any assumptions you find necessary to answer the questions
7. Watch your English, grammar, punctuation and choice of words
8. Time your answers; don't crowd material

8) Answering the essay question

Most essay questions can be answered by framing the specific response around several key words or ideas. Here are a few such key words or ideas:

M's: manpower, materials, methods, money, management
P's: purpose, program, policy, plan, procedure, practice, problems, pitfalls, personnel, public relations

a. Six basic steps in handling problems:
1. Preliminary plan and background development
2. Collect information, data and facts
3. Analyze and interpret information, data and facts
4. Analyze and develop solutions as well as make recommendations
5. Prepare report and sell recommendations
6. Install recommendations and follow up effectiveness

b. Pitfalls to avoid
1. *Taking things for granted* – A statement of the situation does not necessarily imply that each of the elements is necessarily true; for example, a complaint may be invalid and biased so that all that can be taken for granted is that a complaint has been registered

2. *Considering only one side of a situation* – Wherever possible, indicate several alternatives and then point out the reasons you selected the best one
3. *Failing to indicate follow up* – Whenever your answer indicates action on your part, make certain that you will take proper follow-up action to see how successful your recommendations, procedures or actions turn out to be
4. *Taking too long in answering any single question* – Remember to time your answers properly

## IX. AFTER THE TEST

Scoring procedures differ in detail among civil service jurisdictions although the general principles are the same. Whether the papers are hand-scored or graded by machine we have described, they are nearly always graded by number. That is, the person who marks the paper knows only the number – never the name – of the applicant. Not until all the papers have been graded will they be matched with names. If other tests, such as training and experience or oral interview ratings have been given, scores will be combined. Different parts of the examination usually have different weights. For example, the written test might count 60 percent of the final grade, and a rating of training and experience 40 percent. In many jurisdictions, veterans will have a certain number of points added to their grades.

After the final grade has been determined, the names are placed in grade order and an eligible list is established. There are various methods for resolving ties between those who get the same final grade – probably the most common is to place first the name of the person whose application was received first. Job offers are made from the eligible list in the order the names appear on it. You will be notified of your grade and your rank as soon as all these computations have been made. This will be done as rapidly as possible.

People who are found to meet the requirements in the announcement are called "eligibles." Their names are put on a list of eligible candidates. An eligible's chances of getting a job depend on how high he stands on this list and how fast agencies are filling jobs from the list.

When a job is to be filled from a list of eligibles, the agency asks for the names of people on the list of eligibles for that job. When the civil service commission receives this request, it sends to the agency the names of the three people highest on this list. Or, if the job to be filled has specialized requirements, the office sends the agency the names of the top three persons who meet these requirements from the general list.

The appointing officer makes a choice from among the three people whose names were sent to him. If the selected person accepts the appointment, the names of the others are put back on the list to be considered for future openings.

That is the rule in hiring from all kinds of eligible lists, whether they are for typist, carpenter, chemist, or something else. For every vacancy, the appointing officer has his choice of any one of the top three eligibles on the list. This explains why the person whose name is on top of the list sometimes does not get an appointment when some of the persons lower on the list do. If the appointing officer chooses the second or third eligible, the No. 1 eligible does not get a job at once, but stays on the list until he is appointed or the list is terminated.

## X. HOW TO PASS THE INTERVIEW TEST

The examination for which you applied requires an oral interview test. You have already taken the written test and you are now being called for the interview test – the final part of the formal examination.

You may think that it is not possible to prepare for an interview test and that there are no procedures to follow during an interview. Our purpose is to point out some things you can do in advance that will help you and some good rules to follow and pitfalls to avoid while you are being interviewed.

*What is an interview supposed to test?*

The written examination is designed to test the technical knowledge and competence of the candidate; the oral is designed to evaluate intangible qualities, not readily measured otherwise, and to establish a list showing the relative fitness of each candidate – as measured against his competitors – for the position sought. Scoring is not on the basis of "right" and "wrong," but on a sliding scale of values ranging from "not passable" to "outstanding." As a matter of fact, it is possible to achieve a relatively low score without a single "incorrect" answer because of evident weakness in the qualities being measured.

Occasionally, an examination may consist entirely of an oral test – either an individual or a group oral. In such cases, information is sought concerning the technical knowledges and abilities of the candidate, since there has been no written examination for this purpose. More commonly, however, an oral test is used to supplement a written examination.

*Who conducts interviews?*

The composition of oral boards varies among different jurisdictions. In nearly all, a representative of the personnel department serves as chairman. One of the members of the board may be a representative of the department in which the candidate would work. In some cases, "outside experts" are used, and, frequently, a businessman or some other representative of the general public is asked to serve. Labor and management or other special groups may be represented. The aim is to secure the services of experts in the appropriate field.

However the board is composed, it is a good idea (and not at all improper or unethical) to ascertain in advance of the interview who the members are and what groups they represent. When you are introduced to them, you will have some idea of their backgrounds and interests, and at least you will not stutter and stammer over their names.

*What should be done before the interview?*

While knowledge about the board members is useful and takes some of the surprise element out of the interview, there is other preparation which is more substantive. It *is* possible to prepare for an oral interview – in several ways:

**1) Keep a copy of your application and review it carefully before the interview**

This may be the only document before the oral board, and the starting point of the interview. Know what education and experience you have listed there, and the sequence and dates of all of it. Sometimes the board will ask you to review the highlights of your experience for them; you should not have to hem and haw doing it.

**2) Study the class specification and the examination announcement**

Usually, the oral board has one or both of these to guide them. The qualities, characteristics or knowledges required by the position sought are stated in these documents. They offer valuable clues as to the nature of the oral interview. For example, if the job involves supervisory responsibilities, the announcement will usually indicate that knowledge of modern supervisory methods and the qualifications of the candidate as a supervisor will be tested. If so, you can expect such questions, frequently in the form of a hypothetical situation which you are expected to solve. NEVER go into an oral without knowledge of the duties and responsibilities of the job you seek.

**3) Think through each qualification required**

Try to visualize the kind of questions you would ask if you were a board member. How well could you answer them? Try especially to appraise your own knowledge and background in each area, *measured against the job sought*, and identify any areas in which you are weak. Be critical and realistic – do not flatter yourself.

**4) Do some general reading in areas in which you feel you may be weak**

For example, if the job involves supervision and your past experience has NOT, some general reading in supervisory methods and practices, particularly in the field of human relations, might be useful. Do NOT study agency procedures or detailed manuals. The oral board will be testing your understanding and capacity, not your memory.

**5) Get a good night's sleep and watch your general health and mental attitude**

You will want a clear head at the interview. Take care of a cold or any other minor ailment, and of course, no hangovers.

*What should be done on the day of the interview?*

Now comes the day of the interview itself. Give yourself plenty of time to get there. Plan to arrive somewhat ahead of the scheduled time, particularly if your appointment is in the fore part of the day. If a previous candidate fails to appear, the board might be ready for you a bit early. By early afternoon an oral board is almost invariably behind schedule if there are many candidates, and you may have to wait. Take along a book or magazine to read, or your application to review, but leave any extraneous material in the waiting room when you go in for your interview. In any event, relax and compose yourself.

The matter of dress is important. The board is forming impressions about you – from your experience, your manners, your attitude, and your appearance. Give your personal appearance careful attention. Dress your best, but not your flashiest. Choose conservative, appropriate clothing, and be sure it is immaculate. This is a business interview, and your appearance should indicate that you regard it as such. Besides, being well groomed and properly dressed will help boost your confidence.

Sooner or later, someone will call your name and escort you into the interview room. *This is it.* From here on you are on your own. It is too late for any more preparation. But remember, you asked for this opportunity to prove your fitness, and you are here because your request was granted.

*What happens when you go in?*

The usual sequence of events will be as follows: The clerk (who is often the board stenographer) will introduce you to the chairman of the oral board, who will introduce you to the other members of the board. Acknowledge the introductions before you sit down. Do not be surprised if you find a microphone facing you or a stenotypist sitting by. Oral interviews are usually recorded in the event of an appeal or other review.

Usually the chairman of the board will open the interview by reviewing the highlights of your education and work experience from your application – primarily for the benefit of the other members of the board, as well as to get the material into the record. Do not interrupt or comment unless there is an error or significant misinterpretation; if that is the case, do not hesitate. But do not quibble about insignificant matters. Also, he will usually ask you some question about your education, experience or your present job – partly to get you to start talking and to establish the interviewing "rapport." He may start the actual questioning, or turn it over to one of the other members. Frequently, each member undertakes the questioning on a particular area, one in which he is perhaps most competent, so you can expect each member to participate in the examination. Because time is limited, you may also expect some rather abrupt switches in the direction the questioning takes, so do not be upset by it. Normally, a board member will not pursue a single line of questioning unless he discovers a particular strength or weakness.

After each member has participated, the chairman will usually ask whether any member has any further questions, then will ask you if you have anything you wish to add. Unless you are expecting this question, it may floor you. Worse, it may start you off on an extended, extemporaneous speech. The board is not usually seeking more information. The question is principally to offer you a last opportunity to present further qualifications or to indicate that you have nothing to add. So, if you feel that a significant qualification or characteristic has been overlooked, it is proper to point it out in a sentence or so. Do not compliment the board on the thoroughness of their examination – they have been sketchy, and you know it. If you wish, merely say, "No thank you, I have nothing further to add." This is a point where you can "talk yourself out" of a good impression or fail to present an important bit of information. Remember, *you close the interview yourself.*

The chairman will then say, "That is all, Mr. ______, thank you." Do not be startled; the interview is over, and quicker than you think. Thank him, gather your belongings and take your leave. Save your sigh of relief for the other side of the door.

*How to put your best foot forward*

Throughout this entire process, you may feel that the board individually and collectively is trying to pierce your defenses, seek out your hidden weaknesses and embarrass and confuse you. Actually, this is not true. They are obliged to make an appraisal of your qualifications for the job you are seeking, and they want to see you in your best light. Remember, they must interview all candidates and a non-cooperative candidate may become a failure in spite of their best efforts to bring out his qualifications. Here are 15 suggestions that will help you:

**1) Be natural – Keep your attitude confident, not cocky**

If you are not confident that you can do the job, do not expect the board to be. Do not apologize for your weaknesses, try to bring out your strong points. The board is interested in a positive, not negative, presentation. Cockiness will antagonize any board member and make him wonder if you are covering up a weakness by a false show of strength.

**2) Get comfortable, but don't lounge or sprawl**

Sit erectly but not stiffly. A careless posture may lead the board to conclude that you are careless in other things, or at least that you are not impressed by the importance of the occasion. Either conclusion is natural, even if incorrect. Do not fuss with your clothing, a pencil or an ashtray. Your hands may occasionally be useful to emphasize a point; do not let them become a point of distraction.

**3) Do not wisecrack or make small talk**

This is a serious situation, and your attitude should show that you consider it as such. Further, the time of the board is limited – they do not want to waste it, and neither should you.

**4) Do not exaggerate your experience or abilities**

In the first place, from information in the application or other interviews and sources, the board may know more about you than you think. Secondly, you probably will not get away with it. An experienced board is rather adept at spotting such a situation, so do not take the chance.

**5) If you know a board member, do not make a point of it, yet do not hide it**

Certainly you are not fooling him, and probably not the other members of the board. Do not try to take advantage of your acquaintanceship – it will probably do you little good.

**6) Do not dominate the interview**

Let the board do that. They will give you the clues – do not assume that you have to do all the talking. Realize that the board has a number of questions to ask you, and do not try to take up all the interview time by showing off your extensive knowledge of the answer to the first one.

**7) Be attentive**

You only have 20 minutes or so, and you should keep your attention at its sharpest throughout. When a member is addressing a problem or question to you, give him your undivided attention. Address your reply principally to him, but do not exclude the other board members.

**8) Do not interrupt**

A board member may be stating a problem for you to analyze. He will ask you a question when the time comes. Let him state the problem, and wait for the question.

**9) Make sure you understand the question**

Do not try to answer until you are sure what the question is. If it is not clear, restate it in your own words or ask the board member to clarify it for you. However, do not haggle about minor elements.

**10) Reply promptly but not hastily**

A common entry on oral board rating sheets is "candidate responded readily," or "candidate hesitated in replies." Respond as promptly and quickly as you can, but do not jump to a hasty, ill-considered answer.

**11) Do not be peremptory in your answers**

A brief answer is proper – but do not fire your answer back. That is a losing game from your point of view. The board member can probably ask questions much faster than you can answer them.

**12) Do not try to create the answer you think the board member wants**

He is interested in what kind of mind you have and how it works – not in playing games. Furthermore, he can usually spot this practice and will actually grade you down on it.

**13) Do not switch sides in your reply merely to agree with a board member**

Frequently, a member will take a contrary position merely to draw you out and to see if you are willing and able to defend your point of view. Do not start a debate, yet do not surrender a good position. If a position is worth taking, it is worth defending.

**14) Do not be afraid to admit an error in judgment if you are shown to be wrong**

The board knows that you are forced to reply without any opportunity for careful consideration. Your answer may be demonstrably wrong. If so, admit it and get on with the interview.

**15) Do not dwell at length on your present job**

The opening question may relate to your present assignment. Answer the question but do not go into an extended discussion. You are being examined for a *new* job, not your present one. As a matter of fact, try to phrase ALL your answers in terms of the job for which you are being examined.

*Basis of Rating*

Probably you will forget most of these "do's" and "don'ts" when you walk into the oral interview room. Even remembering them all will not ensure you a passing grade. Perhaps you did not have the qualifications in the first place. But remembering them will help you to put your best foot forward, without treading on the toes of the board members.

Rumor and popular opinion to the contrary notwithstanding, an oral board wants you to make the best appearance possible. They know you are under pressure – but they also want to see how you respond to it as a guide to what your reaction would be under the pressures of the job you seek. They will be influenced by the degree of poise you display, the personal traits you show and the manner in which you respond.

ABOUT THIS BOOK

This book contains tests divided into Examination Sections. Go through each test, answering every question in the margin. We have also attached a sample answer sheet at the back of the book that can be removed and used. At the end of each test look at the answer key and check your answers. On the ones you got wrong, look at the right answer choice and learn. Do not fill in the answers first. Do not memorize the questions and answers, but understand the answer and principles involved. On your test, the questions will likely be different from the samples. Questions are changed and new ones added. If you understand these past questions you should have success with any changes that arise. Tests may consist of several types of questions. We have additional books on each subject should more study be advisable or necessary for you. Finally, the more you study, the better prepared you will be. This book is intended to be the last thing you study before you walk into the examination room. Prior study of relevant texts is also recommended. NLC publishes some of these in our Fundamental Series. Knowledge and good sense are important factors in passing your exam. Good luck also helps. So now study this Passbook, absorb the material contained within and take that knowledge into the examination. Then do your best to pass that exam.

# EXAMINATION SECTION

# EXAMINATION SECTION
# TEST 1

DIRECTIONS: Each question or incomplete statement is followed by several suggested answers or completions. Select the one that BEST answers the question or completes the statement. *PRINT THE LETTER OF THE CORRECT ANSWER IN THE SPACE AT THE RIGHT.*

Questions 1-6.

DIRECTIONS: Questions 1 through 6 are to be answered on the basis of the following list of items permitted in cells.

| ITEMS PERMITTED IN CELLS | |
|---|---|
| comb | mop |
| spoon | towel |
| cup | letters |
| envelopes | pen |
| broom | soap |
| washcloth | money |
| writing paper | chair |
| books | dustpan |
| toothpaste | brushes |
| toothbrush | pencil |

The questions consist of sets of pictures of four objects labeled A, B, C, and D. Choose the one object that is NOT in the above list of items permitted and mark its letter in the space at the right. Disregard any information you may have about what is or is not permitted in any institution. Base your answers SOLELY on the above list. Mark only one answer for each question.

1. 1.____

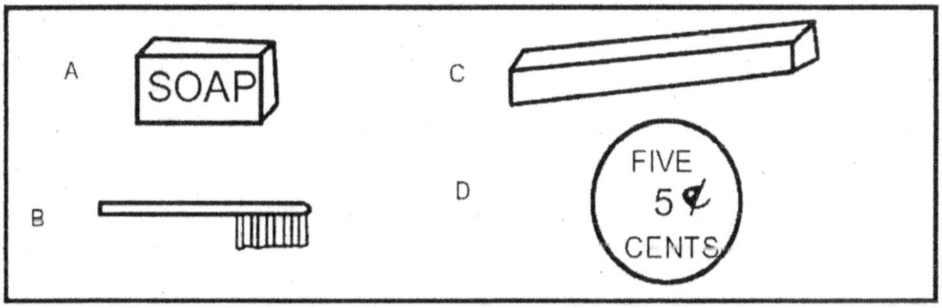


2. 2.____

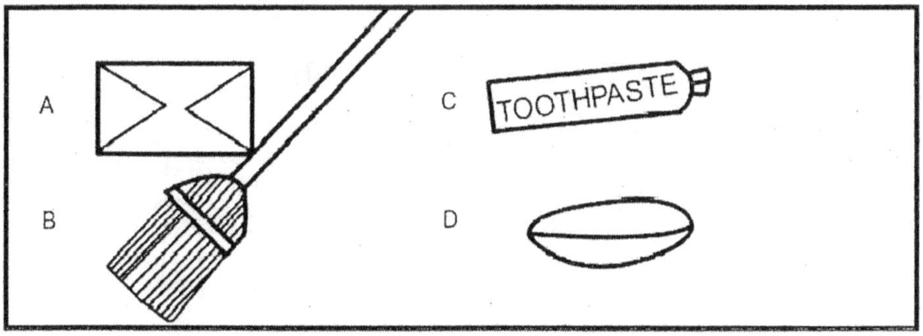

3. 3.____

A

B
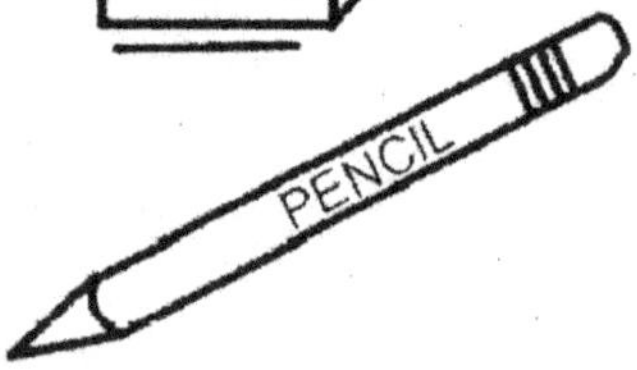


C

D

4. 4.____

A

B

C

D

5. 5.____

A
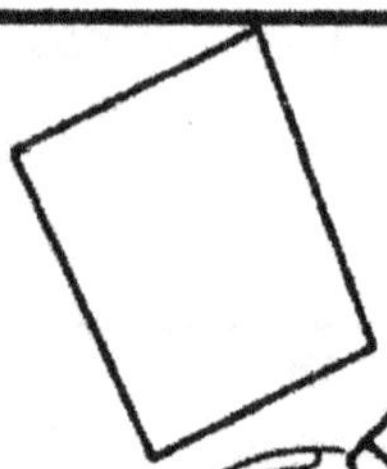

B

C
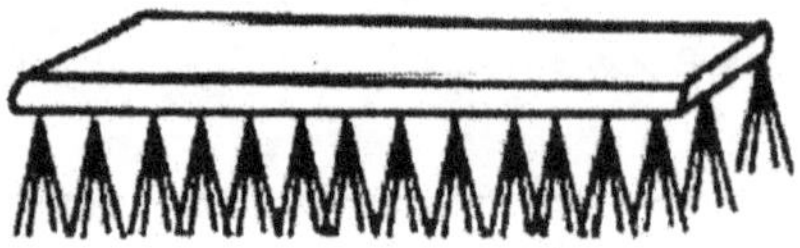

D
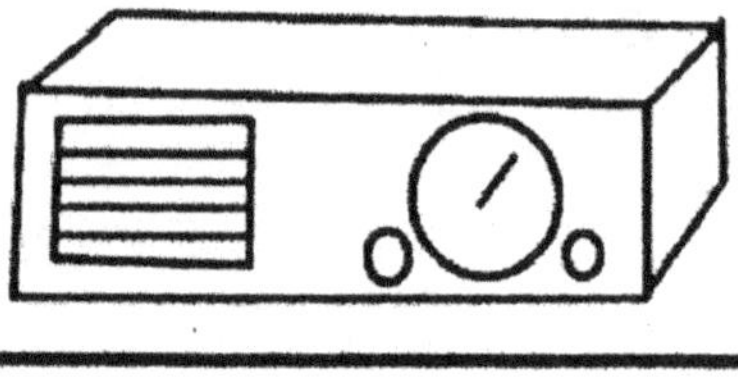

6. 6.____

A
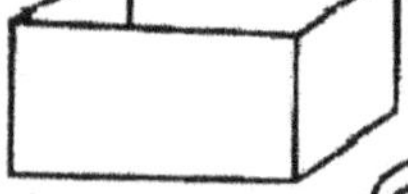

B
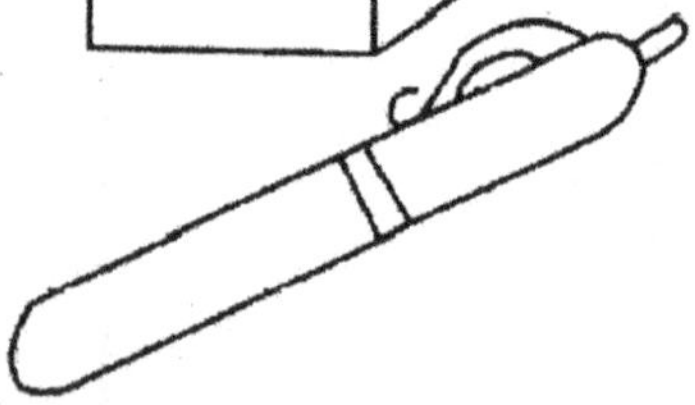

C

D
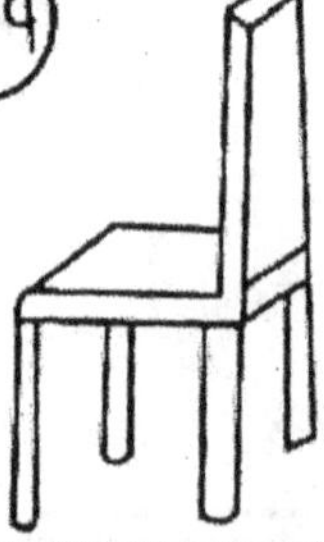

Questions 7-11.

DIRECTIONS: Questions 7 through 11 are to be answered on the basis of the following list showing the name and number of each of nine inmates.

| | | |
|---|---|---|
| 1 - Johnson | 4 - Thompson | 7 - Gordon |
| 2 - Smith | 5 - Frank | 8 - Porter |
| 3 - Edwards | 6 - Murray | 9 - Lopez |

Each question consists of 3 sets of numbers and letters.
Each set should consist of the numbers of three inmates and the first letter of each of their names. The letters should be in the same order as the numbers. In at least two of the three choices, there will be an error.

In the space at the right, mark only that choice in which the letters correspond with the numbers and are in the same order. If all three sets are wrong, mark Choice D in the space at the right.

SAMPLE QUESTION: A. 386 EPM
B. 542 FST
C. 474 LGT

Since 3 corresponds to E for Edwards, 8 corresponds to P for Porter, and 6 corresponds to M for Murray, Choice A is correct and should be entered in the answer space. Choice B is wrong because letters T and S have been reversed. Choice C is wrong because the first number, which is 4, does NOT correspond with the first letter of Choice C, which is L. It should have been T. If Choice A were also wrong, then D would have been the correct answer.

7. A. 382 EGS B. 461 TMJ C. 875 PLF 7.____

8. A. 549 FLT B. 692 MJS C. 758 GSP 8.____

9. A. 936 LEM B. 253 FSE C. 147 JTL 9.____

10. A. 569 PML B. 716 GJP C. 842 PTS 10.____

11. A. 356 FEM B. 198 JPL C. 637 MEG 11.____

Questions 12-16.

DIRECTIONS: Questions 12 through 16 are to be answered on the basis of the following passage.

*Mental disorders are found in a fairly large number of the inmates in correctional institutions. There are no exact figures as to the number of inmates who are mentally disturbed—partly because it is hard to draw a precise line between "mental disturbance" and "normality"—but experts find that somewhere between 15% and 25% of inmates are suffering from disorders that are obvious enough to show up in routine psychiatric examinations. Society has not yet really come to grips with the problem of what to do with mentally disturbed offenders. There is not enough money available to set up treatment programs for all the people identified as mentally disturbed; and there would probably not be enough qualified psychiatric personnel available to run such programs even if they could be set up. Most mentally disturbed offenders are therefore left to serve out their time in correctional institutions, and the burden of dealing with them falls on correction officers. This means that a correction officer must be sensitive enough to human behavior to know when he is dealing with a person who is not mentally normal, and that the officer must be imaginative enough to be able to sense how an abnormal individual might react under certain circumstances.*

12. According to the above passage, mentally disturbed inmates in correctional institutions 12.____

    A. are usually transferred to mental hospitals when their condition is noticed
    B. cannot be told from other inmates because tests cannot distinguish between insane people and normal people
    C. may constitute as much as 25% of the total inmate population
    D. should be regarded as no different from all the other inmates

13. The above passage says that today the job of handling mentally disturbed inmates is MAINLY up to 13.____

    A. psychiatric personnel
    B. other inmates
    C. correction officers
    D. administrative officials

14. Of the following, which is a reason given in the above passage for society's failure to provide adequate treatment programs for mentally disturbed inmates? 14.____

    A. Law-abiding citizens should not have to pay for fancy treatment programs for citizens.
    B. A person who breaks the law should not expect society to give him special help.
    C. It is impossible to tell whether an inmate is mentally disturbed.
    D. There are not enough trained people to provide the kind of treatment needed.

15. The expression *abnormal individual,* as used in the last sentence of the above passage, refers to an individual who is 15.____

    A. of average intelligence
    B. of superior intelligence
    C. completely normal
    D. mentally disturbed

16. The reader of the above passage would MOST likely agree that 16.____

    A. correction officers should not expect mentally disturbed persons to behave the same way a normal person would behave
    B. correction officers should not report infractions
    C. of the rules committed by mentally disturbed persons
    D. mentally disturbed persons who break the law should be treated exactly the same way as anyone else
    E. mentally disturbed persons who have broken the law should not be imprisoned

Questions 17-23.

DIRECTIONS: Questions 17 through 23 are to be answered on the basis of the roster of inmates, the instructions, the table, and the sample question given below.

*Twelve inmates of a correctional institution are divided into three permanent groups in their workshop. They must be present and accounted for in these groups at the beginning of each workday. During the day, the inmates check out of their groups for various activities.*

*They check back in again when those activities have been completed. Assume that the day is divided into three activity periods.*

ROSTER OF INMATES

| | | | | |
|---|---|---|---|---|
| GROUP X | Ted | Frank | George | Harry |
| GROUP Y | Jack | Ken | Larry | Mel |
| GROUP Z | Phil | Bob | Sam | Vic |

*The following table shows the movements of these inmates from their groups during the day. Assume that all were present and accounted for at the beginning of Period I.*

| | | GROUP X | GROUP Y | GROUP Z |
|---|---|---|---|---|
| Period I | Check-outs | Ted, Frank | Ken, Larry | Phil |
| Period II | Check- ins | Frank | Ken, Larry | Phil |
| | Check-outs | George | Jack, Mel | Bob, Sam, Vic |
| Period III | Check-ins | George | Mel, Jack | Sam, Bob, Vic |
| | Check-outs | Frank, Harry | Ken | Vic |

<u>SAMPLE QUESTION</u>: At the end of Period II, the inmates remaining in Group X were

A. Ted, Frank, Harry
B. Frank, Harry
C. Ted, George
D. Frank, Harry, George

During Period I, Ted and Frank were checked out from Group X. During Period II, Frank was checked back in, and George was checked out. Therefore, the members of the group remaining out are Ted and George. The two other members of the group, Frank and Harry, should be present. The correct answer is B.

17. At the end of Period I, the TOTAL number of inmates remaining in their own permanent groups was 17.____

A. 8 B. 7 C. 6 D. 5

18. At the end of Period I, the inmates remaining in Group Z were 18.____

A. George and Harry
B. Jack and Mel
C. Bob, Sam, and Vic
D. Phil

19. At the end of Period II, the inmates remaining in Group Y were 19.____

A. Ken and Larry
B. Jack, Ken, and Mel
C. Jack and Ken
D. Ken, Mel, and Larry

20. At the end of Period II, the TOTAL number of inmates remaining in their own permanent groups was 20.____

A. 8 B. 7 C. 6 D. 5

21. At the end of Period II, the inmates who were NOT present in Group Z were 21.____

A. Phil, Bob, and Sam
B. Sam, Bob, and Vic
C. Sam, Vic, and Phil
D. Vic, Phil, and Bob

22. At the end of Period III, the inmates remaining in Group Y were 22.____

A. Ted, Frank, and George
B. Jack, Mel, and Ken
C. Jack, Larry, and Mel
D. Frank and Harry

23. At the end of Period III, the TOTAL number of inmates NOT present in their own permanent groups was 23.____

A. 4
B. 5
C. 6
D. 7

24. Of the 100 inmates in a certain cellblock, one-half were assigned to clean-up work, and one-fifth were assigned to work in the laundry.
How many inmates were NOT assigned for clean-up work or laundry work? 24.____

A. 30
B. 40
C. 50
D. 60

25. A certain cellblock has a maximum capacity of 250 inmates. On March 26, there were 200 inmates housed in the cellblock. 12 inmates were added on that day, and 17 inmates were added on the following day. No inmates left on either day.
How many more inmates could this cellblock have accommodated on the second day? 25.____

A. 11
B. 16
C. 21
D. 28

---

# KEY (CORRECT ANSWERS)

1. C
2. D
3. A
4. B
5. D

6. A
7. B
8. D
9. A
10. C

11. C
12. C
13. C
14. D
15. D

16. A
17. B
18. C
19. A
20. D

21. B
22. C
23. B
24. A
25. C

---

# TEST 2

DIRECTIONS: Each question or incomplete statement is followed by several suggested answers or completions. Select the one that BEST answers the question or completes the statement. *PRINT THE LETTER OF THE CORRECT ANSWER IN THE SPACE AT THE RIGHT.*

Questions 1-5.

DIRECTIONS: Questions 1 through 5 are to be answered SOLELY on the basis of the Report of Offense that appears below.

| | | | |
|---|---|---|---|
| REPORT OF OFFENSE | | Report No. | *26743* |
| | | Date of Report | *10-12* |
| Inmate | *Joseph Brown* | | |
| Age | *27* | Number | *61274* |
| Sentence | *90 days* | Assignment | *KU-187* |
| Place of Offense | *R.P.W. 4-1* | Date of Offense | *10/11* |
| Offense | *Assaulting inmate* | | |
| Details | *During 9:00 p.m. cellblock clean-up, inmate John Jones asked for pail being used by Brown. Brown refused. Correction officer requested that Brown comply. Brown then threw pail at Jones with intent to injure him and said he would "get" Jones. Jones not hurt.* | | |
| Force Used by Officer | *None* | | |
| Name of Reporting Officer | *R. Rodriguez* | No. | *C-2056* |
| Name of Superior Officer | *P. Ferguson* | | |

1. The person who made out this report is 1.____

   A. Joseph Brown B. John Jones
   C. R. Rodriguez D. P. Ferguson

2. Disregarding the details, the specific offense reported was 2.____

   A. insulting a fellow inmate
   B. assaulting a fellow inmate
   C. injuring a fellow inmate
   D. disobeying a correction officer

3. The number of the inmate who committed the offense is 3.____

   A. 26743 B. 61274 C. KU-187 D. C-2056

4. The offense took place on 4.____

   A. October 11 B. June 12
   C. December D. November 13

5. The place where the offense occurred is identified in the report as 5.____

   A. Brown's cell B. Jones' cell
   C. KU-187 D. R.P.W., 4-1

6. Add $51.79, $29.39, and $8.98. 6.____
The CORRECT answer is

A. $78.97 B. $88.96 C. $89.06 D. $90.16

7. Add $72.07 and $31.54, then subtract $25.75. 7.____
The CORRECT answer is

A. $77.86 B. $82.14 C. $88.96 D. $129.36

8. Start with $82.47, then subtract $25.50, $4.75, and 35¢. 8.____
The CORRECT answer is

A. $30.60 B. $51.87 C. $52.22 D. $65.25

9. Add $19.35 and $37.75, then subtract $9.90 and $19.80. 9.____
The CORRECT answer is

A. $27.40 B. $37.00 C. $37.30 D. $47.20

10. Multiply $38.85 by 2; then subtract $27.90. 10.____
The CORRECT answer is

A. $21.90 B. $48.70 C. $49.80 D. $50.70

11. Add $53.66, $9.27, and $18.75, then divide by 2. 11.____
The CORRECT answer is

A. $35.84 B. $40.34 C. $40.84 D. $41.34

12. Out of 192 inmates in a certain cellblock, 96 are to go on a work detail and another 32 are to report to a vocational class. All the rest are to remain in the cellblock. 12.____
How many inmates should be left on the cellblock?

A. 48 B. 64 C. 86 D. 128

13. Assume that you, as a correction officer, are responsible for seeing that the right number of utensils are counted out for a meal. You need enough utensils for 620 men. One fork and one spoon are needed for each man. In addition, one ladle is needed for each group of 20 men. 13.____
How many utensils will be needed altogether?

A. 1240 B. 1271 C. 1550 D. 1860

14. Assume that you, as a correction officer, are supervising the inmates who are assigned to a dishwashing detail. There is a direct relationship between the amount of time it takes to do all the dishwashing and the number of inmates who are washing dishes. When two inmates are washing dishes, the job takes six hours. 14.____
If there are four inmates washing dishes, how long should the job take?
_______ hour(s).

A. 1 B. 2 C. 3 D. 4

15. Assume that you, as a correction officer, are in charge of supervising the laundry sorting and counting. You expect that on a certain day there will be nearly 7,000 items to be sorted and counted. 15.____
If one inmate can sort and count 500 items in an hour, how many inmates are needed to sort all 7,000 items in one hour?

A. 2 B. 5 C. 7 D. 14

16. A carpentry course is being given for inmates who want to learn a skill. The course will be taught in several different groups. Each group should contain at least 12 but not more than 16 men. The smaller the group, the better, as long as there are at least 12 men per group. If 66 inmates are going to take the course, they should be divided into 16.____

A. 4 groups of 16 men
B. 4 groups of 13 men and 1 group of 14 men
C. 3 groups of 13 men and 2 groups of 14 men
D. 6 groups of 11 men

Questions 17-21.

DIRECTIONS: Questions 17 through 21 are to be answered on the basis of the Fact Situation and the Report of Inmate Injury form below. The questions ask how the report form should be filled in, based on the information given in the Fact Situation.

FACT SITUATION

*Peter Miller is a correction officer assigned to duty in Cellblock A. His superior officer is John Doakes. Miller was on duty at 1:30 P.M. on March 21, 2004, when he heard a scream for help from Cell 12. He hurried to Cell 12 and found inmate Richard Rogers stamping out a flaming book of matches. Inmate John Jones was screaming. It seems that Jones had accidentally set fire to the entire book of matches while lighting a cigarette, and he had burned his left hand. Smoking was permitted at this hour. Miller reported the incident by phone, and Jones was escorted to the dispensary where his hand was treated at 2:00 P.M. by Dr. Albert Lorillo. Dr. Lorillo determined that Jones could return to his cellblock, but that he should be released from work for four days. The doctor scheduled a re-examination for March 22. A routine investigation of the incident was made by James Lopez. Jones confirmed to this officer that the above statement of the situation was correct.*

REPORT OF INMATE INJURY

(1) Name of Inmate ____________ (2) Assignment ____________
(3) Number ____________ (4) Location ____________
(5) Nature of Injury ____________ (6) Date ____________
(7) Details (how, when, where injury was incurred) ____________

(8) Received medical attention: Date ________ Time ________
(9) Treatment ____________
(10) Disposition ( check one or more):
___ (10-1) Return to housing area ___ (10-2) Return to duty
___ (10-3) Work release ____ ____ days ___ (10-4) Re-examine in ____ days

(11) Employing reporting injury ____________
(12) Employee's supervisor or superior officer ____________
(13) Medical officer treating injury ____________
(14) Investigating officer ____________
(15) Head of institution ____________

17. Which of the following should be entered in Item 1? 17.____

A. Peter Miller
B. John Doakes
C. Richard Rogers
D. John Jones

18. Which of the following should be entered in Item 11? 18.____

A. Peter Miller
B. James Lopez
C. Richard Rogers
D. John Jones

19. Which of the following should be entered in Item 8? 19.____

A. 2/21/04, 1:30 P.M.
B. 2/21/04, 2:00 P.M.
C. 3/21/04, 1:30 P.M.
D. 3/21/04, 2:00 P.M.

20. For Item 10, which of the following should be checked? 20.____

A. Only 10-4
B. 10-1 and 10-4
C. 10-1, 10-3, and 10-4
D. 10-2, 10-3, and 10-4

21. Of the following items, which one CANNOT be filled in on the basis of the information given in the Fact Situation? 21.____
Item ______.

A. 12 B. 13 C. 14 D. 15

Questions 22-25.

DIRECTIONS: Questions 22 through 25 are to be answered on the basis of the chart which appears on the following page. The chart shows an 8-hour schedule for 4 groups of inmates. The numbers across the top of the chart stand for hours of the day: the hour beginning at 8:00, the hour beginning at 9:00, and so forth. The exact number of men in each group is given at the lefthand side of the chart. An hour when the men in a particular group are scheduled to be OUT of their cellblock is marked with an X.

| | 8 | 9 | 10 | 11 | 12 | 1 | 2 | 3 |
|---|---|---|---|---|---|---|---|---|
| GROUP Q 44 men | X | | X | | | X | | |
| GROUP R 60 men | X | | X | X | | X | X | |
| GROUP S 24 men | X | | | | X | | | |
| GROUP T 28 men | X | | X | | X | | | |

22. How many of the men were in their cellblock from 11:00 to 12:00? 22.____

A. 60 B. 96 C. 104 D. 156

23. At 10:45, how many of the men were NOT in their cellblock? 23.____

A. 24 B. 60 C. 96 D. 132

24. At 12:30, what proportion of the men were NOT in their cellblock? 24.____

A. 1/4 B. 1/3 C. 1/2 D. 2/3

25. During the period covered in the chart, what percentage of the time did the men in Group S spend in their cellblock? 25.____

A. 60% B. 65% C. 70% D. 75%

---

# KEY (CORRECT ANSWERS)

1. C
2. B
3. B
4. A
5. D
6. D
7. A
8. B
9. A
10. C
11. C
12. B
13. B
14. C
15. D
16. B
17. D
18. A
19. D
20. C
21. D
22. B
23. D
24. B
25. D

# EXAMINATION SECTION
# TEST 1

DIRECTIONS: Each question or incomplete statement is followed by several suggested answers or completions. Select the one that BEST answers the question or completes the statement. *PRINT THE LETTER OF THE CORRECT ANSWER IN THE SPACE AT THE RIGHT.*

Questions 1-25.

DIRECTIONS: Questions 1 through 25 describe situations which might occur in a correctional institution. The institution houses its inmates in cells divided into groups called cellblocks. In answering the questions, assume that you are a correction officer.

1. *Correction officers are often required to search inmates and the various areas of the correctional institution for any items which may be considered dangerous or which are not permitted. In making a routine search, officers should not neglect to examine an item just because it is usually regarded as a permitted item. For instance, some innocent-looking object can be converted into a weapon by sharpening one of its parts or replacing a part with a sharpened or pointed blade.* 1.____

   Which of the following objects could MOST easily be converted into a weapon in this way? A

   A. ballpoint pen
   B. pad of paper
   C. crayon
   D. handkerchief

2. *Only authorized employees are permitted to handle keys. Under no circumstances should an inmate be permitted to use door keys. When not in use, all keys are to be deposited with the security officer.* 2.____

   Which one of the following actions does NOT violate these regulations?

   A. A correction officer has given a trusted inmate the key to a supply room and sends the inmate to bring back a specific item from that room.
   B. A priest comes to make authorized visits to inmates. The correction officer is very busy, so he gives the priest the keys needed to reach certain groups of cells.
   C. An inmate has a pass to go to the library. A cellblock officer examines the pass, then unlocks the door and lets the inmate through.
   D. At the end of the day, a correction officer puts his keys in the pocket of his street clothes and takes them home with him.

3. *Decisions about handcuffing or restraining inmates are often up to the correction officers involved. However, an officer is legally responsible for exercising good judgment and for taking necessary precautions to prevent harm both to the inmate involved and to others.* 3.

   In which one of the following situations is handcuffing or other physical restraint MOST likely to be needed?

A. An inmate seems to have lost control of his senses and is banging his fists repeatedly against the bars of his cell.
B. During the past two weeks, an inmate has deliberately tried to start three fights with other inmates.
C. An inmate claims to be sick and refuses to leave his cell for a scheduled meal.
D. During the night, an inmate begins to shout and sing, disturbing the sleep of other inmates.

4. *Some utensils that are ordinarily used in a kitchen can also serve as dangerous weapons – for instance, vegetable parers, meat saws, skewers, and icepicks. These should be classified as extremely hazardous.* 4.____

The MOST sensible way of solving the problems caused by the use of these utensils in a correctional institution is to

A. try to run the kitchen without using any of these utensils
B. provide careful supervision of inmates using such utensils in the kitchen
C. assign only trusted inmates to kitchen duty and let them use the tools without regular supervision
D. take no special precautions since inmates are not likely to think of using these commonplace utensils as weapons

5. *Inmates may try to conceal objects that can be used as weapons or as escape devices. Therefore, routine searches of cells or dormitories are necessary for safety and security.* 5.____

Of the following, it would probably be MOST effective to schedule routine searches to take place

A. on regular days and always at the same time of day
B. on regular days but at different times of day
C. at frequent but irregular intervals, always at the same time of day
D. at frequent but irregular intervals and at different times of day

6. *One of the purposes of conducting routine searches for forbidden items is to discourage inmates from acquiring such items in the first place. Inmates should soon come to realize that only possessors of these items have reason to fear or resent such searches.* 6.____

Inmates are MOST likely to come to this realization if

A. the searching officer leaves every inmate's possessions in a mess to make it clear that a search has taken place
B. the searching officer confiscates something from every cell, though he may later return most of the items
C. other inmates are not told when a forbidden item is found in an inmate's possession
D. all inmates know that possession of a forbidden item will result in punishment

7. Suppose you are a correction officer supervising a work detail of 22 inmates. All 22 checked in at the start of the work period. Making an informal count an hour later, you count only 21 inmates. 7.____
What is the FIRST action to take?

A. Count again to make absolutely sure how many inmates are present.
B. Report immediately that an inmate has escaped.
C. Try to figure out where the missing inmate could be.
D. Wait until the end of the work period and then make a formal roll call.

8. *The officer who is making a count at night when inmates are in bed must make sure he sees each man. The rule "see living breathing flesh" must be followed in making accurate counts.* 8.____

Of the following, which is the MOST likely reason for this rule?

A. An inmate may be concealing a weapon in the bed.
B. A bed may be arranged to give the appearance of being occupied even when the inmate is not there.
C. Waking inmates for the count is a good disciplinary measure because it shows them that they are under constant guard.
D. It is important for officers on duty at night to have something to do to keep them busy.

9. *When counting a group of inmates on a work assignment, great care should be taken to insure accuracy. The count method should be adapted to the number of inmates and to the type of location.* 9.____

Suppose that you are supervising 15 inmates working in a kitchen. Most of them are moving about constantly, carrying dishes and equipment from one place to another. In order to make an accurate count, which of the following methods would be MOST suitable under these circumstances?

A. Have the inmates *freeze* where they are whenever you call for a count, even though some of them may be carrying hot pans or heavy stacks of dishes.
B. Have the inmates stop their work and gather in one place whenever it is necessary to make a count.
C. Circulate among the inmates and make an approximate count while they are working.
D. Divide the group into sections according to type of work and assign one inmate in each group to give you the number for this section.

10. *Officers on duty at entrances must exercise the greatest care to prevent movement of unauthorized persons. At vehicle entrances, all vehicles must be inspected and a record kept of their arrival and departure.* 10.____

Assume that, as a correction officer, you have been assigned to duty at a vehicle entrance. Which of the following is probably the BEST method of preventing the movement of unauthorized persons in vehicles?

A. If passenger identifications are checked when vehicle enters, no check is necessary when the vehicle leaves.
B. Passenger identifications should be checked for all vehicles when vehicle enters and when it leaves.

C. Passenger identifications need not be checked when vehicle enters, but should always be checked when vehicle leaves.
D. Except for official vehicles, passenger identifications should be checked when vehicle enters and when it leaves.

11. In making a routine search of an inmate's cell, an officer finds various items. Although there is no immediate danger, he is not sure whether the inmate is permitted to have one of the items. 11.____
Of the following, the BEST action for the officer to take is to

A. confiscate the item immediately
B. give the inmate the benefit of the doubt, and let him keep the item
C. consult his rule book or his supervising officer to find out whether the inmate is permitted to have the item
D. leave the item in the inmate's cell, but plan to report him for an infraction of the rules

12. *It is almost certain that there will be occasional escape attempts or an occasional riot or disturbance that requires immediate emergency action. A well-developed emergency plan for dealing with these events includes not only planning for prevention and control and planning for action during the disturbance, but also planning steps that should be taken when the disturbance is over.* 12.____

When a disturbance is ended, which of the following steps should be taken FIRST?

A. Punishing the ringleaders.
B. Giving first aid to inmates or other persons who were injured.
C. Making an institutional count of all inmates.
D. Adopting further security rules to make sure such an incident does not occur again.

13. *It is often important to make notes about an occurrence that will require a written report or personal testimony.* 13.____

Assume that a correction officer has made the following notes for the warden of the institution about a certain occurrence: *10:45 A.M. March 16, 2007. Cellblock A. Robert Brown was attacked by another inmate and knocked to the floor. Brown's head hit the floor hard. He was knocked out. I reported a medical emergency. Dr. Thomas Nunez came and examined Brown. The doctor recommended that Brown be transferred to the infirmary for observation. Brown was taken to the infirmary at 11:15 A.M.*
Which of the following important items of information is MISSING or is INCOMPLETE in these notes? The

A. time that the incident occurred
B. place where the incident occurred
C. names of both inmates involved in the fight
D. name of the doctor who made the medical examination

14. A correction officer has made the following notes for the warden of his institution about an incident involving an infraction of the rules: *March 29, 2007. Cellblock B-4. Inmates involved were A. Whitman, T. Brach, M. Purlin, M. Verey. Whitman and Brach started the trouble around 7:30 P.M. I called for assistance. Officer Haley and Officer Blair responded. Officer Blair got cut, and blood started running down his face. The bleeding looked very bad. He was taken to the hospital and needed eight stitches.* 14.____
Which of the following items of information is MISSING or is INCOMPLETE in these notes?

A. The time and date of the incident
B. The place of the incident
C. Which inmates took part in the incident
D. What the inmates did that broke the rules

15. Your supervising officer has instructed you to follow a new system for handling inmate requests. It seems to you that the new system is not going to work very well and that inmates may resent it. 15.____
What should you do?

A. Continue handling requests the old way but do not let your supervising officer know you are doing this.
B. Continue using the old system until you have a chance to discuss the matter with your supervising officer.
C. Begin using the new system but plan to discuss the matter with your supervising officer if the system really does not work well.
D. Begin using the new system but make sure the inmates know that it is not your idea and you do not approve of it.

16. *Inmates who are prison-wise may know a good many tricks for putting something over. For instance, it is an officer's duty to stop fights among inmates. Therefore, inmates who want to distract the officer's attention from something that is going on in one place may arrange for a phony fight to take place some distance away.* 16.____

To avoid being taken in by a trick like this, a correction officer should

A. ignore any fights that break out among inmates
B. always make an inspection tour to see what is going on elsewhere before breaking up a fight
C. be alert for other suspicious activity when there is any disturbance
D. refuse to report inmates involved in a fight if the fight seems to have been phony

17. *Copies of the regulations are posted at various locations in the cellblock so that inmates can refer to them.* 17.____

Suppose that one of the regulations is changed and the correction officers receive revised copies to post in their cellblocks.
Of the following, the MOST effective way of informing the inmates of the revision is to

A. let the inmates know that you are taking down the old copies and putting up new ones in their place
B. post the new copies next to the old ones so that inmates will be able to compare them and learn about the change for themselves

C. leave the old copies up until you have had a chance to explain the change to each inmate
D. post the new copies in place of the old ones and also explain the change orally to the inmates

18. *A fracture is a broken bone. In a simple fracture, the skin is not broken. In a compound fracture, a broken end of the bone pierces the skin. Whenever a fracture is feared, the first thing to do is to prevent motion of the broken part.* 18.____

Suppose that an inmate has just tripped on a stairway and twisted his ankle. He says it hurts badly, but you cannot tell what is wrong merely by looking at it.
Of the following, the BEST action to take is to

A. tell the inmate to stand up and see whether he can walk
B. move the ankle gently to see whether you can feel any broken ends of bones
C. tell the inmate to rest a few minutes and promise to return later to see whether his condition has improved
D. tell the inmate not to move his foot and put in a call for medical assistance

19. *It is part of institutional procedure that at specified times during each 24-hour period all inmates in the institution are counted simultaneously. Each inmate must be counted at a specific place at a specified time. All movement of inmates ceases from the time the count starts until it is finished and cleared as correct.* 19.____

Assume that, as a correction officer, you are making such a count when an inmate in your area suddenly remembers he has an important 9 A.M. clinic appointment. You check his clinic pass and find that this is true.
What should you do?

A. Let him go to the clinic even though he may be counted again there.
B. Take him off your count and tell him to be sure he is included in the count being made at the clinic.
C. Keep him in your count and tell him to inform the officer at the clinic that he has already been counted.
D. Ask him to wait a few minutes until the counting period is over and then let him go to the clinic.

20. *Except in the case of a serious illness or injury (when a doctor should see the inmate immediately), emergency sick calls should be kept to a minimum, and inmates should be encouraged to wait for regular sick-call hours.* 20.____

In which of the following cases is an emergency sick call MOST likely to be justified?
A(n)

A. inmate has had very severe stomach pains for several hours
B. inmate has cut his hand, and the bleeding has now stopped
C. inmate's glasses have been broken, and he is nearly blind without them
D. normally healthy inmate has lost his appetite and does not want to eat

21. *People who have lost their freedom are likely to go through periods of depression or to become extremely resentful or unpleasant. A correction officer can help inmates who are undergoing such periods of depression by respecting their feelings and treating them in a reasonable and tactful manner.* 21.____

Suppose that an inmate reacts violently to a single request made in a normal, routine manner by a correction officer. Of the following, which is likely to be the MOST effective way of handling the situation?

A. Point out to the inmate that it is his own fault that he is in jail, and he has nobody to blame for his troubles but himself.
B. Tell the inmate that he is acting childishly and that he had better straighten out.
C. Tell the inmate in a friendly way that you can see he is feeling down, but that he should comply with your request.
D. Let the inmate know that you are going to report his behavior unless he changes his attitude.

22. An inmate tells you, a correction officer, of his concern about the ability of his wife and children to pay for rent and food while he is in the institution. 22.____
Of the following, which is the BEST action to take?

A. Assure him that his wife and children are getting along fine, although you do not actually know this.
B. Put him in touch with the social worker or the correction employee who handles such problems.
C. Offer to lend him money yourself if his family is really in need.
D. Advise him to forget about his family and start concentrating on his own problems.

23. *It is particularly important to notice changes in the general pattern of an inmate's behavior. When an inmate who has been generally unpleasant and who has not spoken to an officer unless absolutely necessary becomes very friendly and cooperative, something has happened, and the officer should take steps to make sure what.* 23.____

Of the following possible explanations for this change in behavior, which one is the LEAST likely to be the real cause?

A. The inmate may be planning some kind of disturbance or escape attempt and is trying to fool the officer.
B. The inmate may be trying to get on the officer's good side for some reason of his own.
C. His friendliness and cooperation may indicate a developing mental illness.
D. He may be overcoming his initial hostile reactions to his imprisonment.

24. As a correction officer, you have an idea about a new way for handling a certain procedure. Your method would require a minor change in the regulations, but you are sure it would be a real improvement. 24.____
The BEST thing for you to do is to

A. discuss the idea with your supervising officer, explaining why it would work better than the present method
B. try your idea on your own cellblock, telling inmates that it is just an experiment and not official

C. attempt to get officers on other cellblocks to use your methods on a strictly unofficial basis
D. forget the whole thing since it might be too difficult to change the regulations

25. *Correction officers assigned to visiting areas have a dual supervisory function since their responsibilities include receiving persons other than inmates, as well as handling inmates. Here, of all places, it is important for an officer to realize that he is acting as a representative of his institution and that what he is doing is very much like public relations work.* 25.____

Assume that you are a correction officer assigned to duty in a visiting area.
Which of the following ways of carrying out this assignment is MOST likely to result in good public relations? You should

A. treat inmates and visitors sternly because this will let them know that the institution does not put up with any nonsense
B. be friendly to inmates but suspicious of visitors
C. be stern with inmates but polite and tactful with visitors
D. treat both inmates and visitors in a polite but tactful way

---

# KEY (CORRECT ANSWERS)

1. A
2. C
3. A
4. B
5. D
6. D
7. A
8. B
9. B
10. B
11. C
12. B
13. C
14. D
15. C
16. C
17. D
18. D
19. D
20. A
21. C
22. B
23. C
24. A
25. D

---

# TEST 2

DIRECTIONS: Each question or incomplete statement is followed by several suggested answers or completions. Select the one that BEST answers the question or completes the statement. *PRINT THE LETTER OF THE CORRECT ANSWER IN THE SPACE AT THE RIGHT.*

Questions 1-5.

DIRECTIONS: Answer Questions 1 through 5 on the basis of the following passage.

*The handling of supplies is an important part of correctional administration. A good deal of planning and organization is involved in purchase, stock control, and issue of bulk supplies to the cell-block. This planning is meaningless, however, if the final link in the chain – the cell-blook officer who is in charge of distributing supplies to the inmates – does not do his job in the proper way. First, when supplies are received, the officer himself should immediately check them or should personally supervise the checking, to make sure the count is correct. Nothing but trouble will result if an officer signs for 200 towels and discovers hours later that he is 20 towels short. Did the 20 towels "disappear," or did they never arrive in the first place? Second, all supplies should be locked up until they are actually distributed. Third, the officer must keep accurate records when supplies are issued. Complaints will be kept to a minimum if the officer makes sure that each inmate has received the supplies to which he is entitled, and if the officer can tell from his records when it is time to reorder to prevent a shortage. Fourth, the officer should either issue the supplies himself or else personally supervise the issuing. It is unfair and unwise to put an inmate in charge of supplies without giving him adequate supervision. A small thing like a bar of soap does not mean much to most people, but it means a great deal to the inmate who cannot even shave or wash up unless he receives the soap that is supposed to be issued to him.*

1. Which one of the following jobs is NOT mentioned by the passage as the responsibility of a cellblock officer? 1.____

    A. Purchasing supplies
    B. Issuing supplies
    C. Counting supplies when they are delivered to the cellblock
    D. Keeping accurate records when supplies are issued

2. The passage says that supplies should be counted when they are delivered. Of the following, which is the BEST way of handling this job? 2.____

    A. The cellblock officer can wait until he has some free time and then count them himself.
    B. An inmate can start counting them right away, even if the cellblock officer cannot supervise his work.
    C. The cellblock officer can personally supervise an inmate who counts the supplies when they are delivered.
    D. Two inmates can count them when they are delivered, supervising each other's work.

3. The passage gives an example concerning a delivery of 200 towels that turned out to be 20 towels short. 3.____
The example is used to show that

   A. the missing towels were stolen
   B. the missing towels never arrived in the first place
   C. it is impossible to tell what happened to the missing towels because no count was made when they were delivered
   D. it does not matter that the missing towels were not accounted for because it is never possible to keep track of supplies accurately

4. The MAIN reason given by the passage for making a record when supplies are issued is that keeping records 4.____

   A. will discourage inmates from stealing supplies
   B. is a way of making sure that each inmate receives the supplies to which he is entitled
   C. will show the officer's superiors that he is doing his job in the proper way
   D. will enable the inmates to help themselves to any supplies they need

5. The passage says that it is unfair to put an inmate in charge of supplies without giving him adequate supervision. 5.____
Which of the following is the MOST likely explanation of why it would be *unfair* to do this?

   A. A privilege should not be given to one inmate unless it is given to all the other inmates too.
   B. It is wrong to make on inmate work when all the others can sit in their cells and do nothing.
   C. The cellblock officer should not be able to get out of doing a job by making an inmate do it for him.
   D. The inmate in charge of supplies could be put under pressure by other inmates to do them *special favors.*

Questions 6-10.

DIRECTIONS: Answer Questions 6 through 10 on the basis of the following passage.

*The typical correction official must make predictions about the probable future behavior of his charges in order to make judgments affecting those individuals. In learning to predict behavior, the results of scientific studies of inmate behavior can be of some use. Most studies that have been made show that older men tend to obey rules and regulations better than younger men, and tend to be more reliable in carrying out assigned jobs. Men who had good employment records on the outside also tend to be more reliable than men whose records show haphazard employment or unemployment. Oddly enough, men convicted of crimes of violence are less likely to be troublemakers than men convicted of burglary or other crimes involving stealth. While it might be expected that first offenders would be much less likely to be troublemakers than men with previous convictions, the difference between the two groups is not very great. It must be emphasized, however, that predictions based on a man's background are only likelihoods – they are never certainties. A successful correction officer learns to give some weight to a man's background, but he should rely even more heavily on his own personal judgment of the individual in question. A good officer will develop in time a kind of sixth sense about human beings that is more reliable than any statistical predictions.*

6. The passage suggests that knowledge of scientific studies of inmate behavior would PROBABLY help the correction officer to 6.____

   A. make judgments that affect the inmates in his charge
   B. write reports on all major infractions of the rules
   C. accurately analyze how an inmate's behavior is determined by his background
   D. change the personalities of the individuals in his charge

7. According to the information in the passage, which one of the following groups of inmates would tend to be MOST reliable in carrying out assigned jobs? 7.____

   A. Older men with haphazard employment records
   B. Older men with regular employment records
   C. Younger men with haphazard employment records
   D. Younger men with regular employment records

8. According to the information in the passage, which of the following are MOST likely to be troublemakers? 8.____

   A. Older men convicted of crimes of violence
   B. Younger men convicted of crimes of violence
   C. Younger men convicted of crimes involving stealth
   D. First offenders convicted of crimes of violence

9. The passage indicates that information about a man's background is 9.____

   A. a sure way of predicting his future behavior
   B. of no use at all in predicting his future behavior
   C. more useful in predicting behavior than a correction officer's expert judgment
   D. less reliable in predicting behavior than a correction officer's expert judgment

10. The passage names two groups of inmates whose behavior might be expected to be quite different, but who in fact behave only slightly differently.
    These two groups are 10.____

    A. older men and younger men
    B. first offenders and men with previous convictions
    C. men with good employment records and men with records of haphazard employment or unemployment
    D. men who obey the rules and men who do not

Questions 11-17.

DIRECTIONS: Questions 11 through 17 are based on the following pictures of objects found in Cells A, B, C, and D in a correctional institution.

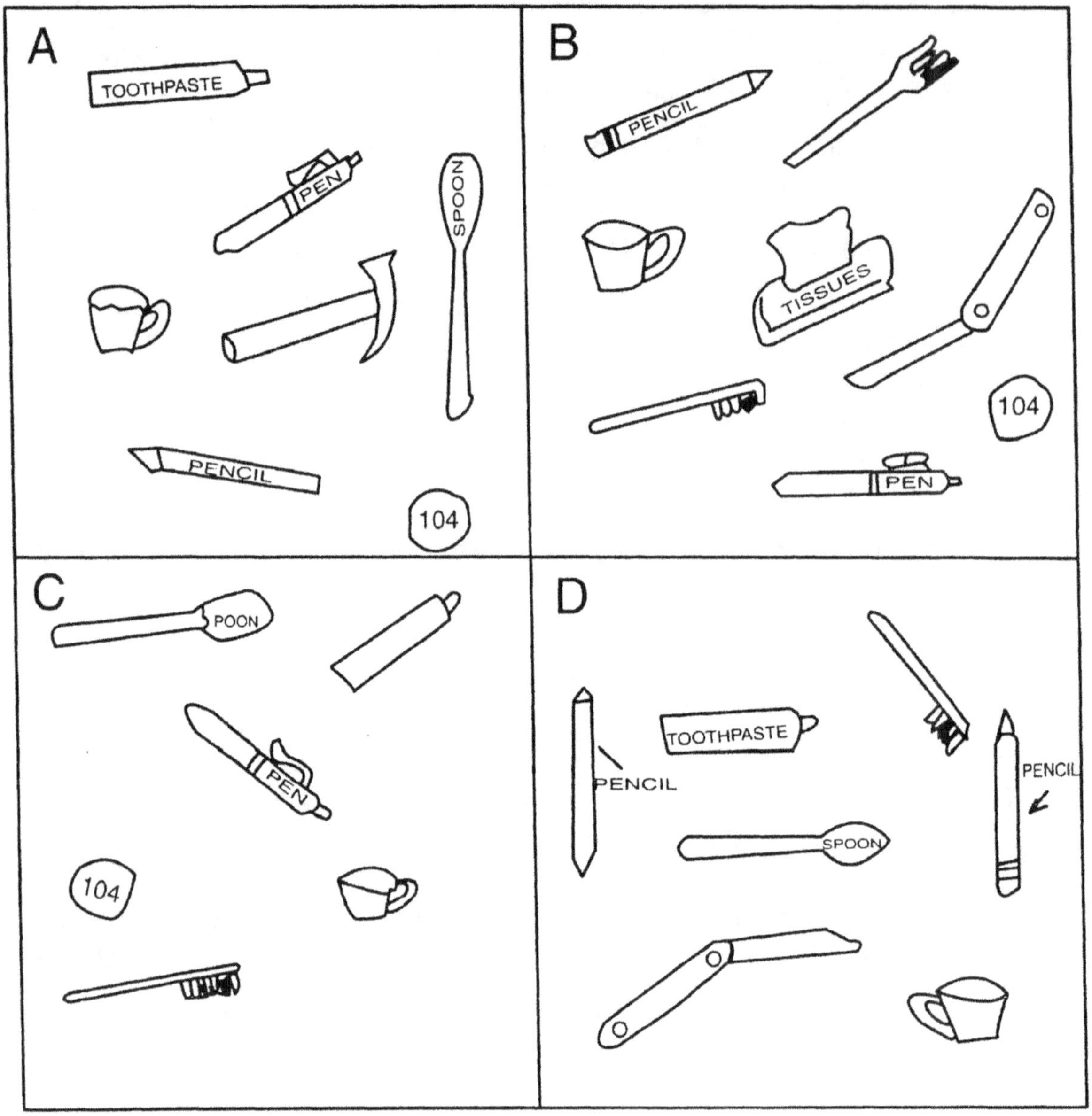


11. Which item can be found in every cell? 11.____

A. Cup B. Money C. Pencil D. Toothpaste

12. Which cell has toothpaste but no toothbrush? 12.____

A. A B. B C. C D. D

13. If knives and forks are prohibited in cells, how many cells are in violation of this rule? 13.____

A. 1 B. 2 C. 3 D. 4

14. One inmate failed to return his tool in the woodworking shop before returning to his cell. That inmate is in Cell 14.____

A. A B. B C. C D. D

15. The cell with the GREATEST number of objects is 15.____

A. A B. B C. C D. D

16. How many cells have AT LEAST one eating utensil? 16.____

A. 1 B. 2 C. 3 D. 4

17. Which cells contain money? 17.____

A. A, B, and C
B. A, B, and D
C. A, C, and D
D. B, C, and D

Questions 18-22.

DIRECTIONS: Answer Questions 18 through 22 on the basis of the following passage.

*A large proportion of the people who are behind bars are not convicted criminals but people who have been arrested and are being held until their trial in court. Experts have often pointed out that this detention system does not operate fairly. For instance, a person who can afford to pay bail usually will not get looked up. The theory of the bail system is that the person will make sure to show up in court when he is supposed to since he knows that otherwise he will forfeit his bail -- he will lose the money he put up. Sometimes a person Who can show that he is a stable citizen with a job and a family will be released on "personal recognizance" (without bail). The result is that the well-to-do, the employed, and the family men can often avoid the detention system. The people who do wind up in detention tend to be the poor, the unemployed, the single, and the young.*

18. According to the above passage, people who are put behind bars 18.____

A. are almost always dangerous criminals
B. include many innocent people who have been arrested by mistake
C. are often people who have been arrested but have not yet come to trial
D. are all poor people who tend to be young and single

19. The passage says that the detention system works *unfairly* against people who are 19.____

A. rich B. married C. old D. unemployed

20. The passage uses the expression *forfeit his bail.* Even if you have not seen the word *forfeit* before, you could figure out from the way it is used in the passage that *forfeiting* probably means ______ something. 20.____

A. losing track of
B. giving up
C. finding
D. avoiding

21. When someone is released on *personal recognizance,* this means that 21.____

A. the judge knows that he is innocent
B. he does not have to show up for a trial
C. he has a record of previous convictions
D. he does not have to pay bail

22. Suppose that two men were booked on the same charge at the same time, and that the same bail was set for both of them. One man was able to put up bail, and he was released. The second man was not able to put up bail, and he was held in detention. The reader of the passage would MOST likely feel that this result is 22.____

A. *unfair,* because it does not have any relation to guilt or innocence
B. *unfair,* because the first man deserves severe punishment
C. *fair,* because the first man is obviously innocent
D. *fair,* because the law should be tougher on poor people than on rich people

23. A certain cellblock has 240 inmates. From 8 A.M. to 9 A.M. on March 25, 120 inmates were assigned to cleanup work, and 25 inmates were sent for physical examinations. All the others remained in their cells. 23.____
How many inmates should have been in their cells during this hour?

A. 65 B. 85 C. 95 D. 105

24. There were 254 inmates in a certain cellblock at the beginning of the day. At 9:30 A.M., 12 inmates were checked out to the dispensary. At 10:00 A.M.,113 inmates were checked out to work details. At 10:30 A.M., 3 inmates were checked out to another cell-block. 24.____
How many inmates were present in this cellblock at 10:45 A.M. if none of the inmates who were checked out had returned?

A. 116 B. 126 C. 136 D. 226

25. There were 242 inmates in a certain cellblock at the beginning of the day. At 9:00 A.M., 116 inmates were checked out to a recreational program. At 9:15 A.M., 36 inmates were checked out to an educational program. At 9:30, 78 inmates were checked out on a work detail. By 10:15, the only inmates who had returned were 115 inmates who had been checked back in from the recreational program. A count made at 10:15 should show that the number of inmates present in the cellblock is 25.____

A. 127 B. 128 C. 135 D. 137

# KEY (CORRECT ANSWERS)

1. A
2. C
3. C
4. B
5. D

6. A
7. B
8. C
9. D
10. B

11. A
12. A
13. B
14. A
15. B

16. D
17. A
18. C
19. D
20. B

21. D
22. A
23. C
24. B
25. A

# EXAMINATION SECTION
# TEST 1

DIRECTIONS: Each question or incomplete statement is followed by several suggested answers or completions. Select the one that BEST answers the question or completes the statement. *PRINT THE LETTER OF THE CORRECT ANSWER IN THE SPACE AT THE RIGHT.*

1. Physical and mental health are essential to the officer. According to this statement, the officer MUST be 1.____

   A. as wise as he is strong
   B. smarter than most people
   C. sound in mind and body
   D. stronger than the average criminal

2. Teamwork is the basis of successful law enforcement. The factor stressed by this statement is 2.____

   A. cooperation
   B. determination
   C. initiative
   D. pride

3. Legal procedure is a means, not an end. Its function is merely to accomplish the enforcement of legal rights. A litigant has no vested interest in the observance of the rules of procedure as such. All that he should be entitled to demand is that he be given an opportunity for a fair and impartial trial of his case. He should not be permitted to invoke the aid of technical rules merely to embarrass his adversary. 3.____
   According to this paragraph, it is MOST correct to state that

   A. observance of the rules of procedure guarantees a fair trial
   B. embarrassment of an adversary through technical rules does not make a fair trial
   C. a litigant is not interested in the observance of rules of procedure
   D. technical rules must not be used in a trial

4. One theory states that all criminal behavior is taught by a process of communication within small intimate groups. An individual engages in criminal behavior if the number of criminal patterns which he has acquired exceed the number of non-criminal patterns. This statement indicates that criminal behavior is 4.____

   A. learned
   B. instinctive
   C. hereditary
   D. reprehensible

5. The law enforcement staff of today requires training and mental qualities of a high order. The poorly or partially prepared staff member lowers the standard of work, retards his own earning power, and fails in a career meant to provide a livelihood and social improvement. 5.____
   According to this statement,

   A. an inefficient member of a law enforcement staff will still earn a good livelihood
   B. law enforcement officers move in good social circles
   C. many people fail in law enforcement careers
   D. persons of training and ability are essential to a law enforcement staff

6. In any state, no crime can occur unless there is a written law forbidding the act or the omission in question; and even though an act may not be exactly in harmony with public policy, such act is not a crime unless it is expressly forbidden by legislative enactment. According to the above statement, 6.____

   A. a crime is committed with reference to a particular law
   B. acts not in harmony with public policy should be forbidden by law
   C. non-criminal activity will promote public welfare
   D. legislative enactments frequently forbid actions in harmony with public policy

7. The unrestricted sale of firearms is one of the main causes of our shameful crime record. According to this statement, one of the causes of our crime record is 7.____

   A. development of firepower
   B. ease of securing weapons
   C. increased skill in using guns
   D. scientific perfection of firearms

8. Every person must be informed of the reason for his arrest unless he is arrested in the actual commission of a crime. Sufficient force to effect the arrest may be used, but the courts frown on brutal methods. According to this statement, a person does not have to be informed of the reason for his arrest if 8.____

   A. brutal force was not used in effecting it
   B. the courts will later turn the defendant loose
   C. the person arrested knows force will be used if necessary
   D. the reason for it is clearly evident from the circumstances

9. An important duty of an officer is to keep order in the court. On the basis of this statement, it is probably true that 9.____

   A. it is more important for an officer to be strong than it is for him to be smart
   B. people involved in court trials are noisy if not kept in check
   C. not every duty of an officer is important
   D. the maintenance of order is important for the proper conduct of court business

10. Ideally, a correctional system should include several types of institutions to provide different degrees of custody. On the basis of this statement, one could MOST reasonably say that 10.____

    A. as the number of institutions in a correctional system increases, the efficiency of the system increases
    B. the difference in degree of custody for the inmate depends on the types of institutions in a correctional system
    C. the greater the variety of institutions, the stricter the degree of custody that can be maintained
    D. the same type of correctional institution is not desirable for the custody of all prisoners

11. The enforced idleness of a large percentage of adult men and women in our prisons is one of the direct causes of the tensions which burst forth in riot and disorder. On the basis of this statement, a good reason why inmates should perform daily work of some kind is that 11.____

A. better morale and discipline can be maintained when inmates are kept busy
B. daily work is an effective way of punishing inmates for the crimes they have committed
C. law-abiding citizens must work; therefore, labor should also be required of inmates
D. products of inmates' labor will, in part, pay the cost of their maintenance

12. With industry invading rural areas, the use of the automobile, and the speed of modern communications and transportation, the problems of neglect and delinquency are no longer peculiar to cities but an established feature of everyday life. 12.____
This statement implies MOST directly that

A. delinquents are moving from cities to rural areas
B. delinquency and neglect are found in rural areas
C. delinquency is not as much of a problem in rural areas as in cities
D. rural areas now surpass cities in industry

13. Young men from minority groups, if unable to find employment, become discouraged and hopeless because of their economic position and may finally resort to any means of supplying their wants. 13.____
The MOST reasonable of the following conclusions that may be drawn from this statement only is that

A. discouragement sometimes leads to crime
B. in general, young men from minority groups are criminals
C. unemployment turns young men from crime
D. young men from minority groups are seldom employed

14. To prevent crime, we must deal with the possible criminal long before he reaches the prison. Our aim should be not merely to reform the law breakers but to strike at the roots of crime: neglectful parents, bad companions, unsatisfactory homes, selfishness, disregard for the rights of others, and bad social conditions. 14.____
The above statement recommends

A. abolition of prisons
B. better reformatories
C. compulsory education
D. general social reform

15. There is evidence which shows that comic books which glorify the criminal and criminal acts have a distinct influence in producing young criminals. 15.____
According to this statement,

A. comic books affect the development of criminal careers
B. comic books specialize in reporting criminal acts
C. young criminals read comic books exclusively
D. young criminals should not be permitted to read comic books

16. Suppose a study shows that juvenile delinquents are equal in intelligence but three school grades behind juvenile non-delinquents. 16.____
On the basis of this information only, it is MOST reasonable to say that

A. a delinquent usually progresses to the educational limit set by his intelligence
B. educational achievement depends on intelligence only
C. educational achievement is closely associated with delinquency
D. lack of intelligence is closely associated with delinquency

17. There is no proof today that the experience of a prison sentence makes a better citizen of an adult. On the contrary, there seems some evidence that the experience is an unwholesome one that frequently confirms the criminality of the inmate. 17.____
From the above paragraph only, it may be BEST concluded that

A. prison sentences tend to punish rather than rehabilitate
B. all criminals should be given prison sentences
C. we should abandon our penal institutions
D. penal institutions are effective in rehabilitating criminals

18. Some courts are referred to as *criminal* courts while others are known as *civil* courts. 18.____
This distinction in name is MOST probably based on the

A. historical origin of the court
B. link between the court and the police
C. manner in which the judges are chosen
D. type of cases tried there

19. Many children who are exposed to contacts and experiences of a delinquent nature become educated and trained in crime in the course of participating in the daily life of the neighborhood. 19.____
From this statement only, we may reasonably conclude that

A. delinquency passes from parent to child
B. neighborhood influences are usually bad
C. schools are training grounds for delinquents
D. none of the above conclusions is reasonable

20. Old age insurance, for whose benefits a quarter of a million city employees may elect to become eligible, is one feature of the Social Security Act that is wholly administered by the Federal government. 20.____
On the basis of this paragraph only, it may MOST reasonably be inferred that

A. a quarter of a million city employees are drawing old age insurance
B. a quarter of a million city employees have elected to become eligible for old age insurance
C. the city has no part in administering Social Security old age insurance
D. only the Federal government administers the Social Security Act

21. An officer's revolver is a defensive, and not offensive, weapon. 21.____
On the basis of this statement only, an officer should BEST draw his revolver to

A. fire at an unarmed burglar
B. force a suspect to confess
C. frighten a juvenile delinquent
D. protect his own life

22. Prevention of crime is of greater value to the community than the punishment of crime. 22.____
If this statement is accepted as true, GREATEST emphasis should be placed on

A. malingering B. medication
C. imprisonment D. rehabilitation

23. The criminal is rarely or never reformed. Acceptance of this statement as true would mean that GREATEST emphasis should be placed on 23.____

A. imprisonment
B. parole
C. probation
D. malingering

24. The MOST accurate of the following statements about persons convicted of crimes is that 24.____

A. their criminal behavior is almost invariably the result of low intelligence
B. they are almost invariably legally insane
C. they are more likely to come from underprivileged groups than from other groups
D. they have certain facial characteristics which distinguish them from non-criminals

25. Suppose a study shows that the I.Q. (Intelligence Quotient) of prison inmates is 95 as opposed to an I.Q. of 100 for a numerically equivalent civilian group. 25.____
A claim, on the basis of this study, that criminals have a lower I.Q. than non-criminals would be

A. *improper;* prison inmates are criminals who have been caught
B. *proper;* the study was numerically well done
C. *improper;* the sample was inadequate
D. *proper;* even misdemeanors are sometimes penalized by prison sentences

Questions 26-45.

DIRECTIONS: In answering Questions 26 through 45, select the letter of the word or expression that MOST NEARLY expresses the meaning of the capitalized word in the group.

26. ABDUCT 26.____

A. lead B. kidnap C. sudden D. worthless

27. BIAS 27.____

A. ability B. envy C. prejudice D. privilege

28. COERCE 28.____

A. cancel B. force C. rescind D. rugged

29. CONDONE 29.____

A. combine B. pardon C. revive D. spice

30. CONSISTENCY 30.____

A. bravery B. readiness C. strain D. uniformity

31. CREDENCE 31.____

A. belief B. devotion C. resemblance D. tempo

32. CURRENT 32.____

A. backward B. brave C. prevailing D. wary

33. CUSTODY 33.____

A. advisement
B. belligerence
C. guardianship
D. suspicion

34. DEBILITY 34.____

A. deceitfulness
B. decency
C. strength
D. weakness

35. DEPLETE 35.____

A. beg B. empty C. excuse D. fold

36. ENUMERATE 36.____

A. name one by one
B. disappear
C. get rid of
D. pretend

37. FEIGN 37.____

A. allow B. incur C. pretend D. weaken

38. INSTIGATE 38.____

A. analyze B. coordinate C. oppose D. provoke

39. LIABLE 39.____

A. careless
B. growing
C. mistaken
D. responsible

40. PONDER 40.____

A. attack B. heavy C. meditate D. solicit

41. PUGILIST 41.____

A. farmer
B. politician
C. prize fighter
D. stage actor

42. QUELL 42.____

A. explode B. inform C. shake D. suppress

43. RECIPROCAL 43.____

A. mutual B. organized C. redundant D. thoughtful

44. RUSE 44.____

A. burn B. impolite C. rot D. trick

45. STEALTHY 45.____

A. crazed B. flowing C. sly D. wicked

Questions 46-50.

DIRECTIONS: Each of the sentences numbered 46 through 50 may be classified under one of the following four categories:

A. faulty because of incorrect grammar
B. faulty because of incorrect punctuation
C. faulty because of incorrect capitalization or incorrect spelling
D. correct

Examine each sentence carefully to determine under which of the above four options it is best classified. Print the letter of the option in the space at the right which is the BEST of the four suggested above. Each faulty sentence contains but one type of error. Consider a sentence to be correct if it contains none of the types of errors mentioned, even though there may be other correct ways of expressing the same thought.

46. They told both he and I that the prisoner had escaped. 46.____

47. Any superior officer, who, disregards the just complaints of his subordinates, is remiss in the performance of his duty. 47.____

48. Only those members of the national organization who resided in the Middle west attended the conference in Chicago. 48.____

49. We told him to give the investigation assignment to whoever was available. 49.____

50. Please do not disappoint and embarass us by not appearing in court. 50.____

51. Suppose a man falls from a two-story high scaffold and is unconscious. You should 51.____

A. call for medical assistance and avoid moving the man
B. get someone to help you move him indoors to a bed
C. have someone help you walk him around until he revives
D. hold his head up and pour a stimulant down his throat

52. For proper first aid treatment, a person who has fainted should be 52.____

A. doused with cold water and then warmly covered
B. given artificial respiration until he is revived
C. laid down with his head lower than the rest of his body
D. slapped on the face until he is revived

53. If you are called on to give first aid to a person who is suffering from shock, you should 53.____

A. apply cold towels
B. give him a stimulant
C. keep him awake
D. wrap him warmly

54. Artificial respiration would NOT be proper first aid for a person suffering from 54.____

A. drowning
B. electric shock
C. external bleeding
D. suffocation

55. Suppose you are called on to give first aid to several victims of an accident. FIRST attention should be given to the one who is 55.____

A. bleeding severely
B. groaning loudly
C. unconscious
D. vomiting

56. If an officer's weekly salary is increased from $480 to $540, then the percent of increase is _______ percent. 56.____

A. 10
B. 11 1/9
C. 12 1/2
D. 20

57. Suppose that one-half the officers in a department have served for more than ten years, and one-third have served for more than 15 years. 57.____
Then, the fraction of officers who have served between ten and fifteen years is

A. 1/3
B. 1/5
C. 1/6
D. 1/12

58. In a city prison, there are four floors on which prisoners are housed. The top floor houses one-quarter of the inmates, the bottom floor houses one-sixth of the inmates, one-third are housed on the second floor. The rest of the inmates are housed on the third floor. 58.____
If there are 90 inmates housed on the third floor, the TOTAL number of inmates housed on all four floors together is

A. 270
B. 360
C. 450
D. 540

59. Suppose that ten percent of those who commit serious crimes are convicted and that fifteen percent of those convicted are sentenced for more than 3 years. 59.____
The percentage of those committing serious crimes who are sentenced for more than 3 years is _______ percent.

A. 15
B. 1.5
C. .15
D. .015

60. Assume that there are 1,100 employees in a city agency. Of these, 15 percent are officers, 80 percent of whom are attorneys. Of the attorneys, two-fifths have been with the agency over five years. 60.____
Then, the number of officers who are attorneys and have over five years' experience with the agency is MOST NEARLY

A. 45
B. 53
C. 132
D. 165

61. An employee who has 500 cartons of supplies to pack can pack them at the rate of 50 an hour. After this employee has worked for half an hour, he is joined by another employee who can pack 45 cartons an hour. 61.____
Assuming that both employees can maintain their respective rates of speed, then the TOTAL number of hours required to pack all the cartons is

A. 4 1/2
B. 5
C. 5 1/2
D. 6 1/2

62. Thirty-six officers can complete an assignment in 22 days. Assuming that all officers work at the same rate of speed, the number of officers that would be needed to complete this assignment in 12 days is 62.____

A. 42
B. 54
C. 66
D. 72

Questions 63-65.

DIRECTIONS: Questions 13 through 15 are to be answered on the basis of the following table. Data for certain categories have been omitted from the table. You are to calculate the missing numbers if needed to answer the questions.

| | 2005 | 2006 | Numerical Increase |
|---|---|---|---|
| Correction Officers | 1,226 | 1,347 | 34 |
| Court Attendants | | 529 | |
| Deputy Sheriffs | 38 | 40 | |
| Supervisors | | | |
| | 2,180 | 2,414 | - |

63. The number in the *Supervisors* group in 2005 was MOST NEARLY 63.____

A. 500 B. 475 C. 450 D. 425

64. The LARGEST percentage increase from 2005 to 2006 was in the group of 64.____

A. Court Officers
B. Court Attendants
C. Deputy Sheriffs
D. Supervisors

65. In 2006, the ratio of the number of Court Officers to the total of the other three categories of employees was MOST NEARLY 65.____

A. 1:1 B. 2:1 C. 3:1 D. 4:1

66. A directed verdict is made by a court when 66.____

A. the facts are not disputed
B. the defendant's motion for a directed verdict has been denied
C. there is no question of law involved
D. neither party has moved for a directed verdict

67. Papers on appeal of a criminal case do NOT include one of the following: 67.____

A. Summons
B. Minutes of trial
C. Complaint
D. Intermediate motion papers

68. A pleading titled *Smith vs. Jones, et. al.* indicates 68.____

A. two plaintiffs
B. two defendants
C. more than two defendants
D. unknown defendants

69. A District Attorney makes a *prima facie* case when 69.____

A. there is proof of guilt beyond a reasonable doubt
B. the evidence is sufficient to convict in the absence of rebutting evidence
C. the prosecution presents more evidence than the defense
D. the defendant fails to take the stand

70. A person is NOT qualified to act as a trial juror in a criminal action if he or she 70.____

A. has been convicted previously of a misdemeanor
B. is under 18 years of age
C. has scruples against the death penalty
D. does not own property of a value at least $500

71. A court clerk who falsifies a court record commits a(n) 71.____

A. misdemeanor
B. offense
C. felony
D. no crime, but automatically forfeits his tenure

72. Insolent and contemptuous behavior to a judge during a court of record proceeding is punishable as 72.____

A. civil contempt
B. criminal contempt
C. disorderly conduct
D. a disorderly person

73. Offering a bribe to a court clerk would not constitute a crime UNLESS the 73.____

A. court clerk accepted the bribe
B. bribe consisted of money
C. bribe was given with intent to influence the court clerk in his official functions
D. court was actually in session

74. A defendant comes to trial in the same court in which he had previously been defendant in a similar case. 74.____
The court officer should

A. tell him, *knew we'd be seeing you again*
B. tell newspaper reporters what he knows of the previous action
C. treat him the same as he would any other defendant
D. warn the judge that the man had previously been a defendant

75. Suppose in conversation with you, an attorney strongly criticizes a ruling of the judge and you believe the attorney to be correct. 75.____
You should

A. assure him you feel the same way
B. tell him the judge knows the law
C. tell him to ask for an exception
D. refuse to discuss the matter

76. One of the inmates in the institution where you are on duty as correction officer is serving a sentence for having molested a small girl. 76.____
You should

A. assume that the man should rightfully be in a mental institution
B. behave towards this man exactly the same as towards the other inmates
C. handle this man somewhat more gently because he is not a dangerous criminal
D. handle this man somewhat roughly because of his contemptible crime

77. Suppose that one inmate attacks another in a washroom in a correctional institution. From this information ONLY, it is safe to infer 77.____

A. that a knife was used in the attack
B. that the attacker was young and strong
C. that the washroom was otherwise empty
D. none of the foregoing

78. Suppose that an inmate is found badly beaten and unconscious in a corner of the prison laundry where he is employed. 78.____
Of the following, the question which would be MOST useful to a correction officer in questioning other inmates to determine the identity of the attacker is:

A. What method of assault was used?
B. When did the assault take place?
C. Who was the assailant?
D. Why was the inmate assaulted?

79. Of the following circumstances, the one a correction officer should LEAST validly regard with suspicion is a(n) 79.____

A. inmate not being in his cell during the regular check before *lights-out*
B. inmate not reporting to his work assignment and who cannot be found
C. visitor's attempt to *sneak* an article to an inmate
D. well-dressed young woman coming to see an inmate during visiting hours

80. Suppose you are the correction officer in charge of a work group of about 15 inmates in the institutional garage. Of the following, the MOST practical way to prevent the inmates from concealing tools and carrying them back to their cells is to 80.____

A. assign one or more tools to each inmate and hold him responsible for them
B. have a definite place for each tool and check to see that it is there at the end of the day
C. require inmates to strip each day before they are taken back to their cells
D. search each man both at the end and the beginning of each day

81. An inmate stops you and tells you that international bankers are out to *get* him, that already two attempts have been made on his life, and he now fears that the air he breathes is being poisoned. The inmate is an old man who has been in and out of the institution frequently for such minor offenses as vagrancy, alcoholism, loitering, etc. This man is MOST probably 81.____

A. a victim of amnesia
B. a victim of a persecution complex
C. covering up an infraction of the rules
D. the object of an international plot

82. Suppose that while you are off duty and unarmed, you recognize on the street an inmate who escaped from your correctional institution a year ago. Apparently, he does not see or recognize you. During this escape, the inmate had gotten hold of a gun and seriously wounded a correction officer. 82.____
The BEST of the following actions for you to take is to

A. attack and subdue the man immediately
B. engage the man in conversation to make sure of your identification
C. follow the man until you can summon an officer to your aid
D. shout *escaped prisoner* so that passersby will help you

83. Suppose a correction officer, feeling that the sentence given an inmate was unfair, permits him to escape. 83.____
On the basis of this information ONLY, it is safe to assume that the

A. correction officer used poor judgment
B. correction officer was recently appointed
C. inmate had possession of a large sum of money
D. judge passing sentence was unduly harsh

84. Suppose that a correctional institution is specially constructed to be escape-proof. Nevertheless, two inmates escape. 84.____
The MOST reasonable conclusion on the basis of this information only is that

A. goals are not always successfully attained
B. not all correction officers are honest
C. the escapers were helped by confederates outside
D. two heads are more resourceful than one

85. Which one of the following descriptions of an escaped inmate would be MOST effective in helping to recapture him? 85.____

A. Age - 31 years; weight - 168 pounds
B. At time of escape was wearing gray hat, dark overcoat
C. Deep scar running from left ear to chin
D. Height - 5 feet, 9 inches; complexion - sallow

86. Allowing inmates to read newspapers in their spare time is 86.____

A. *desirable* since they should be kept informed of the news
B. *undesirable* since they will read of crimes they can imitate after release
C. *desirable* since the advertisements will make them more ambitious
D. *undesirable* since they will read of prison escapes elsewhere

87. Suppose an inmate commits an infraction in the mess hall. The MAIN reason why a correction officer might wait until he was back in his cell before reprimanding him would be that 87.____

A. he should be given time to reflect on his error
B. it might interfere with his enjoyment of the meal
C. the correction officer is not busy during meal times
D. there are several hundred other inmates in the mess hall

88. Of the following, the MOST important reason why correction officers should see to it that the inmates under their supervision know and understand the rules and regulations of the institution is that 88.____

A. the inmates will become aware of the punishment for each violation
B. the job of the correction officers will be made much easier

C. unintentional violations of the rules will be reduced
D. with full understanding there will be no violations

89. In considering punishment for an infraction of the rules by an inmate, the disciplinary board in a correction institution is usually guided MAINLY by the thought that 89.____

A. infractions must be punished whether intentional or unintentional
B. most infractions are deliberate and only few are unintentional
C. the aim of punishment is to achieve better individual adjustment of the inmate
D. the infraction was committed by an individual who is a criminal

90. *When an inmate commits an infraction of discipline, the disciplinary officer or board shall hold a hearing and recommend disciplinary action.* 90.____
The punishment that should be reserved for the MOST serious infractions is

A. a severe reprimand before other inmates
B. denial of athletic privileges
C. loss of time off for good behavior
D. restriction against attending movies

91. *Parole boards have gradually taken over from the judges the function of specifying terms of imprisonment because they are usually in a better position to perform this task.* 91.____
The MAIN reason for this is most probably that the parole board

A. can also consider the inmate's prison record
B. has closer contact with the inmate
C. is composed of more than one person
D. usually includes experts in criminology

92. *In the selection of books for the library of a correctional institution, emphasis should be placed on diversified material.* 92.____
The MAIN reason for this is the

A. desire of most inmates to prepare themselves for vocations
B. fact that most inmates come from urban areas
C. interest displayed by most inmates in western fiction
D. various age groups and interests of the inmates

93. Unscheduled or inconstant patrols by officers will frustrate any planned attempt at irregularity on the part of inmates. 93.____
According to the preceding statement, it is MOST reasonable to assume that

A. an officer should carefully follow his patrol schedule
B. inmates should be taught regularity in their activities
C. officers should make their patrol intentions known to inmates
D. the element of surprise should be used by officers in their patrols

94. Generally, the prospect of rehabilitating juvenile delinquents is considerably dimmed by throwing them into the same hopper of criminal procedures and institutions as the adult criminals. Yet, it is a fact that some juvenile offenders are more contaminated by contact with some of their peers than by contact with adult offenders. 94.____
On the basis of the preceding statement, it would be MOST desirable in the correctional treatment of juvenile offenders to

A. classify and segregate all prisoners into groups on the sole basis of type of crime they have committed in order to assure that no undesirable contacts will take place
B. recognize no distinction between juvenile and adult offenders and allow them to mingle throughout the custodial and correctional procedures
C. separate only those adult offenders guilty of the most serious crimes from the general prisoner group and allow the others, adult and juveniles, to mingle throughout the correctional and custodial procedures
D. separate the adults from the juveniles but also further separate the juveniles into groups according to their characteristics

95. It is a frequent misconception that correction officers can be recruited from those registers established for the recruitment of city police or firemen. While it is true that many common qualifications are found in all of these, specific standards for correctional institution work are indicated, varying with the size, geographical location and policies of the institution. 95.____
According to this paragraph only, it may be BEST be inferred that

A. a successful correction officer must have some qualifications not required of a policeman or fireman
B. qualifications which make a successful patrolman will also make a successful fireman
C. the same qualifications are required of a correction officer regardless of the institution to which he is assigned
D. the successful correction officer is required to be both more intelligent and stronger than a fireman

96. A correction officer shall not receive a gift from any inmate or other person on the inmate's behalf. 96.____
The BEST explanation for this rule is that

A. acceptance of a gift has no significance
B. favors may be expected in return
C. inmates cannot usually afford gifts
D. gifts are only an expression of good will

97. Correction officers who deal with the inmate who is a habitual offender should have no false impressions about his character. While extending him a square deal, they should always consider him a source of danger. 97.____
According to this statement ONLY, correction officers should deal with inmates who are habitual offenders

A. carefully and fairly
B. courageously and with self-reliance
C. tolerantly and honestly
D. understandingly and with sympathy

98. Regulations do not permit a correction officer to fire a revolver except when absolutely necessary. 98.____
On the basis of this information only, it may be MOST reasonably inferred that

A. ammunition and bullets are too expensive to be used indiscriminately
B. many correction officers have been dismissed for unnecessary use of firearms
C. the cleaning of a firearm after use is a tedious, time-consuming task
D. the use of a revolver by a correction officer may sometimes be harmful

99. Suppose that a study of inmates at a correctional institution shows that a comparatively small number of first offenders become second offenders, but a very high percentage of second offenders commit further crimes. The MOST reasonable of the following conclusions from this information only is that 99.____

A. the average age of first offenders is considerably less than that of second offenders
B. it is more difficult to rehabilitate a second offender than a first offender
C. second offenses are likely to be more serious crimes than first offenses
D. the term *offender,* as used in the study, is scientifically unacceptable

100. For the correction officer, the problem of the feebleminded is one of great importance since this group makes up a large proportion of the offenders in any court or institution. Of the following, the one which is NOT a cause of this large proportion of feebleminded inmates is that 100.____

A. a high percentage of dull offenders are caught and convicted
B. many dull delinquents come from poor environment
C. men with low intelligence have natural criminal tendencies
D. the youth of low intelligence is easily led into crime

# KEY (CORRECT ANSWERS)

| | | | | |
|---|---|---|---|---|
| 1. C | 21. D | 41. C | 61. C | 81. B |
| 2. A | 22. D | 42. D | 62. C | 82. C |
| 3. B | 23. A | 43. A | 63. D | 83. A |
| 4. A | 24. C | 44. D | 64. D | 84. A |
| 5. D | 25. A | 45. C | 65. A | 85. C |
| 6. A | 26. B | 46. A | 66. A | 86. A |
| 7. B | 27. C | 47. B | 67. D | 87. D |
| 8. D | 28. B | 48. C | 68. C | 88. C |
| 9. D | 29. B | 49. D | 69. B | 89. C |
| 10. D | 30. D | 50. C | 70. B | 90. C |
| 11. A | 31. A | 51. A | 71. C | 91. A |
| 12. B | 32. C | 52. C | 72. B | 92. D |
| 13. A | 33. C | 53. D | 73. C | 93. D |
| 14. D | 34. D | 54. C | 74. C | 94. D |
| 15. A | 35. B | 55. A | 75. D | 95. A |
| 16. C | 36. A | 56. C | 76. B | 96. B |
| 17. A | 37. C | 57. C | 77. D | 97. A |
| 18. D | 38. D | 58. B | 78. C | 98. D |
| 19. D | 39. D | 59. B | 79. D | 99. B |
| 20. C | 40. C | 60. B | 80. B | 100. C |

# TEST 2

DIRECTIONS: Each question or incomplete statement is followed by several suggested answers or completions. Select the one that BEST answers the question or completes the statement. *PRINT THE LETTER OF THE CORRECT ANSWER IN THE SPACE AT THE RIGHT.*

1. From the standpoint of progressive prison management, it is desirable that the inmates consider the correction officer as a person interested in their welfare rather than as an opponent MAINLY because 1.____

   A. a favorable attitude toward the officer on the part of inmates will help in their rehabilitation
   B. correction officers must perform their duties without regard to the attitudes which they may develop in the inmates
   C. most people expect the correction officer to treat the inmates kindly
   D. prison personnel are now *correction officers* and not *prison guards*

2. One part of the correction officer's job is to see to it that the inmates obey the rules and regulations of the institution. 2.____
   To succeed in this part of the job, it would be BEST for the correction officer to

   A. get the inmates to agree with the rules they must obey
   B. get the inmates to understand the need for each rule
   C. see that all the inmates know and understand the rules
   D. stress to the inmates all the penalties for violation of the rules

3. The man who is a prisoner today was a free man yesterday and will be a free man again tomorrow. 3.____
   Of the following, the CHIEF significance of this statement for persons engaged in prison work is that

   A. a prisoner should not be treated any better than a person who was never in prison
   B. it is not right to put a man in prison for punishment
   C. prisoners sometimes escape to gain freedom
   D. the prison ought to prepare the inmates for normal living

4. A correction officer shall immediately notify the Department of any change in address. 4.____
   Of the following, the BEST reason for this rule is that it

   A. allows for more efficient assignment of correction officers
   B. gives the supervisor a chance to transfer the officer to a new work location if the present one is far from the officer's home
   C. makes it possible to get in touch with the officer quickly in an emergency
   D. makes record keeping within the Department more efficient

5. Of the following, the crime which a person is LEAST likely to hesitate to commit because of the fear of getting a long prison term is 5.____

   A. burglary of a loft
   B. embezzlement
   C. robbery of a bank
   D. unplanned murder

6. Two correction officers who had successfully kept a possible riot situation in check were praised by their superior for having shown unusual alertness. The officers commented that they had merely followed the procedures outlined in their CORRECTION OFFICER'S MANUAL. 6.____
This incident illustrates that, of the following, the CHIEF value of a good knowledge of their MANUAL for correction officers is that it will help them to

A. carry out their duties most effectively
B. develop an original and unique course of action for each new situation
C. stop possible riots unassisted
D. understand human nature better

7. A correctional institution has other functions besides those of good discipline and secure custody. 7.____
The one of the following which is LEAST directly related to the functions of good discipline and secure custody is the

A. fair and consistent treatment of inmates by prison personnel
B. frequency of careful searches and inspections within the institution
C. institution's efforts to correct the inmate's antisocial tendencies
D. institution's regulations to insure safety

8. Of the following, the MOST important reason for having separate correctional institutions for different types of offenders is that 8.____

A. a smaller staff is required to care for the total prison population when the inmates are separated by type of offense
B. it is easier to give specialized treatment to offenders of the same type when they are housed in a separate institution
C. it is less expensive to build several small, specialized institutions than one large, general institution
D. the judge can sentence the prisoner to a particular institution, relieving the Department of Correction of the responsibility for determining placement

9. At any particular meal, the average prison inmate is likely to be LEAST concerned with the 9.____

A. amount of meat served at the meal
B. freshness and cleanliness of the food
C. nourishment value of the food served
D. warmth of the food when served

10. Courts sometimes sentence convicted offenders to an indefinite term, specifying a minimum and a maximum time which is to be served. 10.____
Of the following, the CHIEF advantage of this type of indeterminate sentence from a correctional point of view is that

A. a prisoner can be released sooner if moral improvement is shown
B. money is saved for the state
C. the actual time to be served is at the discretion of the judge
D. the criminal can thereby be convinced to testify for the state

11. When cloth is purchased to make prison clothing for sentenced inmates, it is LEAST important that the cloth 11.____

A. be fairly priced
B. have good wearing qualities so that it can last a reasonably long time
C. have stripes of a certain width
D. present no special problems in cleaning or laundering

12. Of the following, a factor that may make it difficult for released prisoners to *go straight* is the fact that 12.____

A. lasting reformation must come from within and cannot be imposed from without
B. many of their friends and contacts are members of the underworld
C. scientific advancements have made modern living more pleasant
D. they are given close supervision by the police for several years

13. It is a post-institutional method of treating offenders outside prison walls. 13.____
The preceding definition describes MOST NEARLY

A. bail
B. pardon
C. parole
D. social case work

14. The theory has been advanced that there is, in most cases, a psychological time for the release of each prison inmate when the outlook for his rehabilitation is best. Assuming this theory to be correct, an important reason why it is difficult to put it into practice is that the 14.____

A. follow-up after the inmate's release is as important as his release at the proper time
B. length of an inmate's sentence is set by the judge at the time of sentencing
C. number of cases where the theory does not hold true is quite large
D. psychological time is different for each inmate

15. This man must be a correction officer because he wears a uniform. 15.____
This statement is faulty mainly because it assumes that

A. a man who wears a uniform may be a correction officer
B. a man who wears a uniform may not be a correction officer
C. correction officers wear uniforms
D. only correction officers wear uniforms

16. Black, who is suspected of having stolen some property from Tier A, claims that he could not have stolen the property because his cell is in Tier B. 16.____
In order to prove that Black actually could have stolen the property, it is MOST important to know

A. Black's record at the prison
B. how long it takes to get from Tier B to Tier A
C. if Black could get into Tier A
D. if the stolen property could be of value to Black personally

17. Of the following, the LEAST important reason for censoring incoming mail of prisoners is to 17.____

A. look for any cash money being sent to prisoners
B. look for information which may be the key to an escape plot
C. prevent prisoners from learning of family problems that may worry them
D. prevent the smuggling of drugs into the prison

18. Progressive prison administrators GENERALLY agree that a recreation program for prison inmates 18.____

A. has little value in training prisoners to become better citizens
B. is too expensive to be installed in most prisons
C. reduces considerably the number of officers needed to guard inmates
D. should include other activities besides sports

19. It has been found that the better correction officer makes fewer official complaints against inmates for violations of rules. 19.____
Of the following, the MOST probable reason for this is that the better officer

A. can afford to be more lenient when an inmate commits a violation of the rules
B. has good control of inmates so that occasions for violations do not arise frequently
C. is able to punish an inmate without making an official complaint of the violation
D. knows the proper techniques to use to force inmates to obey the rules

20. A correction officer must take all possible precautions when investigating a fake suicide. 20.____
Of the following, the MOST probable reason for this rule is that

A. failure by an officer to take all possible precautions when investigating a fake suicide will result in the inmate's death
B. inmates sometimes pretend to commit suicide merely to place the officer in a position open to attack
C. the investigation of a suicide is potentially more dangerous to the safety of the officer and the prison than the investigation of many other dangerous situations
D. there are sometimes unexpected opportunities for committing suicide in a prison

21. Of the following, the MOST important reason why an officer assigned to supervise a large group of inmates eating in a mess hall should be especially alert is that 21.____

A. all inmates must finish eating in time to report to their work locations
B. inmates might complain about monotonous or unappetizing food
C. some inmates might complain that they did not receive equal size portions
D. very many inmates in the same place at one time is potentially dangerous

22. Suppose that there is a rule which prohibits inmates of a prison from having any cash money in their possession. Of the following, the LEAST important argument in favor of such a rule is that 22.____

A. it will be easier for inmates to buy things from the prison commissary with cash money
B. it will reduce stealing of money by one inmate from another
C. there will be less gambling among inmates
D. there will be less chance of inmates using cash money to try to bribe employees

23. A correction officer is locking the inmates in their cells for the night. 23.____
Of the following, the BEST way for the officer to make sure that no inmate is missing is to

A. count and identify the inmates before locking them in and then check each cell after locking in
B. have inmates call out their names as they march past on the way to their cells
C. have inmates turn in their names and numbers on slips of paper on the way to their cells
D. line the inmates up, call their names, and check them off as they answer to their names

24. Of the following, the MOST probable reason why a greater number of juvenile delinquents is generally found in a city neighborhood than in a country neighborhood of comparable area is that 24.____

A. a large proportion of the population of cities is made up of *undesirables*
B. the concentration of population in city areas is generally greater than that in country areas
C. the educational methods of cities are not as good as those of the country districts
D. there is greater availability of television, radio, and recreation in city areas

25. When starting to search a prisoner who has been transferred from another institution, a correction officer notices what appear to be a number of small, recently healed punctures in the skin of the prisoner's arm. This discovery should be of significance to the correction officer CHIEFLY as an indication that the prisoner 25.____

A. may have been mistreated at the other institution
B. should be carefully searched for any instruments of self-mutilation
C. should be carefully searched for narcotics
D. should be checked for a history of skin disease

26. A certain correction officer who, upon inspection of a cell, found in it an accumulation of past issues of newspapers, removed all but one or two newspapers from the cell. 26.____
The action of this officer was

A. *good* because such an accumulation is a potential fire hazard
B. *poor* because it deprives the inmate of a form of recreation
C. *good* because the normal interval of time between inspections should be reduced
D. *poor* because the officer could give the extra issues to other inmates

27. Prisoners awaiting trial are not permitted to have razors. Of the following, the MOST important reason for such a rule is that 27.____

A. an inmate who cuts himself with a razor could hold the institution responsible for the injury
B. inmates have no means of buying razors
C. razors may be turned into dangerous weapons
D. trial prisoners are held for such a short time that they do not need shaves

28. Suppose there is a rule that a police officer cannot interview an inmate at the prison unless he presents Form DD-22 from the Police Department. While you are on duty, a detective asks to interview an inmate but claims he left the Form DD-22 at the precinct. Of the following, the BEST action for you to take is to 28.____

A. ask him to be sure to get the Form DD-22 and bring it to you immediately after he finishes interviewing the inmate
B. call the precinct to find out if he left the Form DD-22 there and, if so, permit him to interview the inmate
C. check his official identification to be sure he is a detective, then permit him to interview the inmate
D. refuse to permit him to interview the inmate until he presents Form DD-22

29. Suppose that a thief assumes a new name in order to prevent law enforcement agencies from finding out who he really is.
The assumed name is usually referred to as a(n) 29.____

A. misnomer
B. alias
C. alibi
D. nom de plume

30. Of the following, the MAIN difference in organization or function between the Police Department and the Department of Correction is that the Police Department 30.____

A. catches criminals whereas the Department of Correction keeps them in jail
B. has a semi-military type of organization whereas the Department of Correction has a civilian set-up
C. is headed by a Commissioner whereas a Board of Correction is at the head of the Department of Correction
D. is subject to State supervision whereas the Department of Correction is not

31. Custody in prison work used to be considered of such supreme importance that everything else was secondary. This statement implies MOST directly that 31.____

A. formerly nothing was as important as custody in prison work
B. formerly only custody was considered important in prison work
C. today all aspects of prison work are considered equally important
D. today reform of the prisoner is considered more important than custody

32. Since the total inmate treatment and training program is conditioned largely by custody requirements, its success is almost wholly dependent on flexibility of custody classification and handling of prisoners.
Of the following, the MOST accurate statement based on the preceding statement is that the 32.____

A. conditions of custody are completely dependent on the handling of inmates in accordance with their classification
B. daily schedule at the institution should be flexible in order for the treatment and training program to succeed
C. main factor influencing the inmate treatment and training program is the requirement for the proper safekeeping of inmates
D. most important factor in the success of the treatment and training program is the cooperation of the inmates

33. As the fundamental changes sought to be brought about in the inmates of a correctional institution can be accomplished only under good leadership, it follows that the quality of the staff, whose duty it is to influence and guide the inmates in the right direction, is more important than the physical facilities of the institution. 33.____
Of the following, the MOST accurate conclusion based on the preceding statement is that

A. the development of leadership is the fundamental change brought about in inmates by good quality staff
B. the physical facilities of an institution are not very important in bringing about fundamental changes in the inmates
C. with proper training, the entire staff of a correctional institution can be developed into good leaders
D. without good leadership, the basic changes desired in the inmates of a correctional institution cannot be brought about

34. Prisoners who are receiving decent food and humane treatment and who are busily engaged in useful work programs, carefully organized and purposeful leisure time activities, and self-improvement, rarely resort to disturbances or escape attempts. 34.____
The one of the following that is NOT mentioned in the preceding statement as a factor in reducing escape attempts by prisoners is a

A. program of productive employment
B. proper classification program
C. proper feeding program
D. systematized recreation program

35. Physical punishment of prison inmates has been shown by experience not only to be ineffective but to be dangerous and, in the long run, destructive of good discipline. 35.____
According to the preceding statement, it is MOST reasonable to assume that, in the supervision of prison inmates,

A. a good correction officer would not use physical punishment
B. it is permissible for a good correction officer to use a limited amount of physical punishment to enforce discipline
C. physical punishment improves discipline temporarily
D. the danger of public scandal is basic in cases where physical punishment is used

36. There is no clear evidence that criminals, as a group, differ from non-criminals in their basic psychological needs. 36.____
On the basis of this statement, it is MOST reasonable to assume that criminals and non-criminals

A. are alike in some important respects
B. are alike in their respective backgrounds
C. differ but slightly in all respects
D. differ in physical characteristics

37. Neither immediate protection for the community nor long-range reformation of the prisoner can be achieved by prison personnel who express toward the offender whatever feelings of frustration, fear, jealousy, or hunger for power they may have. 37.____
Of the following, the CHIEF significance of this statement for correction officers is that, in their daily work, they should

A. be on the constant lookout for opportunities to prove their courage to inmates
B. not allow deeply personal problems to affect their relations with the inmates
C. not try to advance themselves on the job because of personal motives
D. spend a good part of their time examining their own feelings in order to understand better those of the inmates

38. Since ninety-five percent of prison inmates are released, and a great majority of these within two to three years, a prison which does nothing more than separate the criminal from society offers little promise of real protection to society. 38.____
Of the following, the MOST valid reference which may be drawn from the preceding statement is that

A. once it has been definitely established that a person has criminal tendencies, that person should be separated for the rest of his life from ordinary society
B. prison sentences in general are much too short and should be lengthened to afford greater protection to society
C. punishment, rather than separation of the criminal from society, should be the major objective of a correctional system
D. when a prison system produces no change in prisoners, and the period of imprisonment is short, the period during which society is protected is also short

39. A great handicap to successful correctional work lies in the negative response of the general community to the offender. Public attitudes of hostility toward, and rejection of, an ex-prisoner can undo the beneficial effects of even an ideal correctional system. 39.____
Of the following, the CHIEF implication of this statement is that

A. a friendly community attitude will insure the successful reformation of the ex-prisoner
B. correctional efforts with most prisoners would generally prove successful if it were not for public hostility toward the former inmate
C. in the long-run, even an ideal correctional system cannot successfully reform criminals
D. the attitude of the community toward an ex-prisoner is an important factor in determining whether or not an ex-prisoner reforms

40. While retribution and deterrence as a general philosophy in correction are widely condemned, no one raises any doubt as to the necessity for secure custody of some criminals. 40.____
Of the following, the MOST valid conclusion based on the preceding statement is that the

A. gradual change in the philosophy of correction has not affected custody practices
B. need for safe custody of some criminals is not questioned by anyone
C. philosophy of retribution, as shown in some correctional systems, has led to wide condemnation of custodial practices applied to all types of criminals
D. practice of secure custody of some criminals is the result of society's desire for retribution and deterrence

Questions 41-42.

DIRECTIONS: Questions 41 and 42 are to be answered on the basis of the following paragraph.

*Those correction theorists who are in agreement with severe and rigid controls as a normal part of the correctional process are confronted with a contradiction; this is so because a responsibility which is consistent with freedom cannot be developed in a repressive atmosphere. They do not recognize this contradiction when they carry out their programs with dictatorial force and expect convicted criminals exposed to such programs to be reformed into free and responsible citizens.*

41. According to the above paragraph, those correction theorists are faced with a contradiction who 41.____

A. are in favor of the enforcement of strict controls in a prison
B. believe that to develop a sense of responsibility, freedom must not be restricted
C. take the position that the development of responsibility consistent with freedom is not possible in a repressive atmosphere
D. think that freedom and responsibility can be developed only in a democratic atmosphere

42. According to the above paragraph, a repressive atmosphere in a prison 42.____

A. does not conform to present day ideas of freedom of the individual
B. is admitted by correction theorists to be in conflict with the basic principles of the normal correctional process
C. is advocated as the best method of maintaining discipline when rehabilitation is of secondary importance
D. is not suitable for the development of a sense of responsibility consistent with freedom

43. To state the matter in simplest terms, just as surely as some people are inclined to commit crimes, so some people are prevented from committing crimes by the fear of the consequences to themselves. 43.____
Of the following, the MOST logical conclusion based on this statement is that

A. as many people are prevented from committing criminal acts as actually commit criminal acts
B. most men are not inclined to commit crimes
C. people who are inclined to violate the law are usually deterred from their purpose
D. there are people who have a tendency to commit crimes and people who are deterred from crime

44. Probation is a judicial instrument whereby a judge may withhold execution of a sentence upon a convicted person in order to give opportunity for rehabilitation in the community under the guidance of an officer of the court. According to the preceding statement, it is MOST reasonable to assume that 44.____

A. a person on probation must report to the court at least once a month
B. a person who has been convicted of crime is sometimes placed on probation by the judge

C. criminals who have been rehabilitated in the community are placed on probation by the court after they are sentenced
D. the chief purpose of probation is to make the sentence easier to serve

Questions 45-47.

DIRECTIONS: Questions 45 through 47 are to be answered on the basis of the information contained in the following paragraph.

*Group counseling may contain potentialities of an extraordinary character for the philosophy and especially the management and operation of the adult correctional institution. Primarily, the change may be based upon the valued and respected participation of the rank-and-file of employees in the treatment program. Group counseling provides new treatment functions for correctional workers. The older, more conventional duties and activities of correctional officers, teachers, maintenance foremen and other employees, which they currently perform, may be fortified and improved by their participation in group counseling. Psychologists, psychiatrists, and classification officers may also need to revise their attitudes toward others on the staff and toward their own procedure in treating inmates to accord with the new type of treatment program which may evolve if group counseling were to become accepted practice in the prison. The primary locale of the psychological treatment program may move from the clinical center to all places in the institution where inmates are in contact with employees. The thoughtful guidance and steering of the program, figuratively its pilot-house, may still be the clinical center. The actual points of contact of the treatment program will, however, be wherever inmates are in personal relationship, no matter how superficial, with employees of the prison.*

45. According to the above paragraph, a basic change that may be brought about by the introduction of a group counseling program into an adult correctional institution would be that the 45.____

A. educational standards for correctional employees would be raised
B. management of the institution would have to be selected primarily on the basis of ability to understand and apply the counseling program
C. older and conventional duties of correctional employees would assume less importance
D. rank-and-file employees would play an important part in the treatment program for inmates

46. According to the above paragraph, the one of the following that is NOT mentioned specifically as a change that may be required by or result from the introduction of group counseling in an adult correctional institution is a change in the 46.____

A. attitude of the institution's classification officers toward their own procedures in treating inmates
B. attitudes of the institution's psychologists toward correction officers
C. place where the treatment program is planned and from which it is directed
D. principal place where the psychological treatment program makes actual contact with the inmate

47. According to the above paragraph, under a program of group counseling in an adult correctional institution, treatment of inmates takes place 47.____

A. as soon as they are admitted to the prison
B. chiefly in the clinical center
C. mainly where inmates are in continuing close and personal relationship with the technical staff
D. wherever inmates come in contact with prison employees

Questions 48-50.

DIRECTIONS: Questions 48 and 50 are to be answered on the basis of the information contained in the following paragraph.

*As a secondary aspect of this revolutionary change in outlook resulting from the introduction of group counseling into the adult correctional institution, there must evolve a new type of prison employee, the true correctional or treatment worker. The top management will have to reorient their attitudes toward subordinate employees, respecting and accepting them as equal participants in the work of the institution. Rank may no longer be the measure of value in the inmate treatment program. Instead, the employee will be valuable whatever his location in the prison hierarchy or administrative plan in terms of his capacity constructively to relate himself to inmates as one human being to another. In group counseling, all employees must consider it their primary task to provide a wholesome environment for personality growth for the inmates in work crews, cell blocks, clerical pools or classrooms. The above does not mean that custodial care and precautions regarding the prevention of disorders or escapes are cast aside or discarded by prison workers. On the contrary, the staff will be more acutely aware of the costs to the inmates of such infractions of institutional rules. Gradually, it is hoped, these instances of uncontrolled responses to over-powering feelings by inmates will become much less frequent in the treatment institution. In general, men in group counseling provide considerably fewer disciplinary infractions when compared with a control group of those still on a waiting list to enter group counseling, and especially fewer than those who do not choose to participate. It is optimistically anticipated that some day men in prison may have the same attitudes toward the staff, the same security in expecting treatment as do patients in a good general hospital.*

48. According to the above paragraph, under a program of group counseling in an adult correctional institution, that employee will be MOST valuable in the inmate treatment program who 48.____

A. can establish a constructive relationship of one human being to another between himself and the inmate
B. gets top management to accept him as an equal participant in the work of the institution
C. is in contact with the inmate in work crews, cell blocks, clerical pools or classrooms
D. provides the inmate with a proper home environment for wholesome personality growth

49. According to the above paragraph, an effect that the group counseling program is expected to have on the problem of custody and discipline in a prison is that the staff will 49.____

A. be more acutely aware of the cost of maintaining strict prison discipline
B. discard old and outmoded notions of custodial care and the prevention of disorders and escapes
C. neglect this aspect of prison work unless proper safeguards are established
D. realize more deeply the harmful effect on the inmate of breaches of discipline

50. According to the above paragraph, a result that is expected from the group counseling method of inmate treatment in an adult correctional institution is 50.____

A. a greater desire on the part of potential delinquents to enter the correctional institution for the purpose of securing treatment
B. a large reduction in the number of infractions of institutional rules by inmates
C. a steady decrease in the crime rate
D. the introduction of hospital methods of organization and operation into the correctional institution

# KEY (CORRECT ANSWERS)

| | | | | |
|---|---|---|---|---|
| 1. A | 11. C | 21. D | 31. A | 41. A |
| 2. C | 12. B | 22. A | 32. C | 42. D |
| 3. D | 13. C | 23. A | 33. D | 43. D |
| 4. C | 14. B | 24. B | 34. B | 44. B |
| 5. D | 15. D | 25. C | 35. A | 45. D |
| 6. A | 16. C | 26. A | 36. A | 46. C |
| 7. C | 17. C | 27. C | 37. B | 47. D |
| 8. B | 18. D | 28. D | 38. D | 48. A |
| 9. C | 19. B | 29. B | 39. D | 49. D |
| 10. A | 20. B | 30. A | 40. B | 50. B |

# EXAMINATION SECTION
# TEST 1

DIRECTIONS: Each question or incomplete statement is followed by several suggested answers or completions. Select the one that BEST answers the question or completes the statement. *PRINT THE LETTER OF THE CORRECT ANSWER IN THE SPACE AT THE RIGHT.*

1. Of the following, it is MOST important that a newly appointed correction officer be 1.____

   A. intelligent
   B. thoroughly informed on the latest correctional techniques
   C. unafraid of anything
   D. very strong

2. The correction officer's attitude toward the prisoners supervised should be very 2.____

   A. friendly
   B. impartial
   C. suspicious
   D. tough

3. Of the following, the BEST reason for separating first offenders from habitual offenders in a prison is that 3.____

   A. contact with hardened inmates may be harmful to the first offender
   B. first offenders may object to being housed with other criminals
   C. first offenders should be sent to reformatories rather than confined in a prison
   D. individual attention should be given to every inmate

4. Of the following, the LEAST important reason for sending law violators to prison is to 4.____

   A. discourage them from committing more crimes in the future
   B. punish them for their violation of the law
   C. remove them from the influence of society
   D. warn other possible offenders that crime does not pay

5. John Jones, who has a long record of juvenile delinquency, is the son of Robert Jones who has a long criminal record. The one of the following which has probably contributed LEAST to making John a juvenile delinquent is 5.____

   A. growth in a poor environment
   B. hero worship
   C. inherited criminal traits
   D. parental neglect

6. Suppose that studies show that 15% of all prison inmates have had no schooling, 67.5% have attended elementary school only, 14.5% have attended high school, and 3% have had some college. 6.____
   On the basis of this data, it is MOST reasonable to assume that

   A. a smaller percentage of college graduates than of high school graduates commit crimes
   B. educational attainment is related to crime as depression is related to unemployment

C. educational opportunities have increased but crime has not decreased
D. people with little education make up the greatest part of the general prison population

7. Of the following, the MAIN reason why it is desirable for a correction officer to know the criminal history of the inmates supervised is that 7.____

A. an inmate's criminal history is a factor influencing the type of custodial supervision the officer must give
B. the inmates will be favorably impressed with the officer's knowledge of the job
C. the officer may be called upon to testify in court about these inmates
D. while many inmates are confined in the one prison, no two inmates will have the same criminal history

8. Sometimes a person who has just been charged with a crime is kept in jail until the trial comes up. The relationship established between the correction officer and such a prisoner who has just been admitted and is waiting to be tried is very important MAINLY because this class of prisoner is usually 8.____

A. aware of the need to abide by prison regulations
B. emotionally upset because of imprisonment
C. in need of legal advice from the correction officer
D. most likely to try to win favor with the correction officer

9. Of the following, the CHIEF value of a brief introductory training course for newly appointed correction officers is that such a course can 9.____

A. give the new employee an introduction to the basic aspects of the correction officer's job
B. give the new employees a thorough knowledge of the main principles of correctional theory and practice
C. point up the relationship of the correction department to other government agencies
D. serve as an additional test of the employees' fitness for the position

10. Suppose you have reason to believe that there is contraband hidden in one or more of the cells on your post. However, after making a quick search, you have been unable to find any contraband. 10.____
Of the following, the BEST action for you to take is to

A. forget about the matter; as your search has failed to locate any contraband, you were probably mistaken
B. keep on the alert for a few months until you catch an inmate using contraband
C. recommend to your captain that a thorough search of the post be organized
D. search the suspected cells again at some time in the future

11. Suppose that you are transferred to a post that has been supervised by another officer for a few years. The daily post routine established by this officer is very different from the one that you would prefer to use. 11.____
In this situation, it would be MOST desirable for you to

A. immediately adopt your own routine so that the inmates will know what to expect
B. introduce changes in routine gradually so that the inmates under your supervision will not be confused
C. let the routine established by the other officer continue unchanged as it has taken a long time to build up
D. make up a new routine consisting of about fifty percent of procedures used by the other officer and fifty percent of procedures that you favor

12. Suppose that a civilian employee of the prison commissary comes to your post to sell small articles to the inmates. The inmates have crowded around the commissary employee, and the selling is taking place in a very disorderly and noisy manner.
Of the following, the MOST desirable action for you to take is to 12.____

A. arrange the inmates in a line and have the commissary items sold to them in line order
B. contact the commissary office and ask them to send up another employee to help with the selling
C. help the commissary employee yourself with the selling so that the inmates can be taken care of more quickly
D. stop the sale of commissary items and tell the commissary employee to come back another time

13. Suppose that the rules of the prison do not allow a prisoner to carry more than a certain amount of cash at any one time. One day you find that a prisoner on your post is carrying more than the allowable amount of cash. Of the following, the BEST action for you to take would be to 13.____

A. have the prisoner turn over the extra cash to you and submit it to your superior with a report
B. issue a warning to the prisoner against further violations of this rule in the future
C. say nothing to the prisoner but keep a close watch to see if the money is spent
D. take away the extra cash and keep it until the prisoner is released

14. Suppose that while you are on duty alone in a mess hall where a fairly large number of inmates are having supper, two inmates walk over to you and in a loud and insulting manner demand more food, claiming that some of their food is spoiled.
Of the following, it would be MOST desirable for you to 14.____

A. give the inmates more food but report them to your superior for disciplinary action after they have been returned to their cells
B. order the inmates back to their table, using force if necessary
C. order the inmates out of the mess hall and back to the cell tier
D. tell the inmates that you will give them more food from the kitchen only if they agree to pay for it later

15. Suppose that an inmate on your post is afraid of an attack by certain other inmates of the cell tier.
Of the following, the BEST action for you to take is to 15.____

A. announce at the next inmate roll call that assault is a misdemeanor even if committed in prison
B. discuss with your immediate superior the advisability of moving this inmate to another floor in the institution

C. immediately take this inmate to see the head of the prison
D. tell the inmate not to be afraid as there is always an officer on guard

16. Suppose that you are in charge of a work gang made up of inmates from different tiers and floors of the prison. Upon taking a count after the work gang is assembled one morning, you find that one prisoner has not yet reported. Of the following, the BEST action for you to take is to 16.____

A. immediately begin a search for the missing prisoner with the help of the other inmates of the work gang
B. notify the head of the prison
C. report this fact by telephone to the officer in command of the tier to which the missing inmate is assigned
D. sound a general alarm

17. One day you take a count of the inmates of your cell block after they return from mess and find that you are one inmate over. 17.____
Of the following, the BEST action for you to take is to

A. ask that anyone who does not belong in this group step forward and let this inmate return to the proper tier
B. assign the extra inmate to a cell and wait until the inmate is reported missing
C. call the roll of the inmates, ask if the name of any inmate has not been called, and then let this inmate return to the proper tier
D. personally identify each inmate against your records in order to first make sure who the extra inmate is

18. A correction officer is alone with a group of inmates at work when two of the inmates start a fight. The officer immediately steps in and tries to separate the two inmates by force. This action is 18.____

A. *desirable* because it keeps the fight from spreading
B. *desirable* because it shows the inmates that the officer is not afraid
C. *undesirable* because it is preferable to let the two inmates fight it out rather than to let the other inmates get out of control
D. *undesirable* because the officer should first call for assistance before taking any further action

19. Of the following, the MAIN reason why it is generally undesirable for a correction officer to reprimand an inmate in front of other inmates is that 19.____

A. discipline should be thought out before it is applied
B. embarrassment may make the inmate resentful and create problems of supervision for the officer
C. the officer should not hesitate to show the other inmates that he is always in command of the situation
D. the other inmates may object to the officer's action because they consider it to be unwarranted

20. Suppose that you are informed by Inmate X that the prisoners on your post have made plans to stage a riot in the mess hall the next day. 20.____
Of the following, the BEST action for you to take is to

A. be especially on the alert the next day so as to forestall any riot that may be planned before it gets started
B. have the probable ringleaders fed in their cells the next day
C. line up the inmates, tell them you have received certain information from Inmate X, and warn them against any forbidden demonstrations
D. notify your commanding officer who will make a decision as to what should be done

21. A correction officer is justified in using physical force against an inmate 21.____

A. in self-defense
B. under no circumstances
C. when no weapons are at hand
D. when provoked by an inmate

22. When entering a cell occupied by an inmate to investigate a suspicious circumstance, a correction officer should be accompanied by another officer. 22.____
This recommendation is

A. *sound* because additional protection is afforded in the event of sudden attack
B. *sound* because additional witnesses to suspicious circumstances must always be produced
C. *unsound* because it is wasteful of staff
D. *unsound* because serious delay will occur if another officer is not immediately available

23. Reading of newspapers, books, or other materials by a correction officer while on duty is prohibited. 23.____
Of the following, the BEST justification for this rule is that the

A. material read cannot be thoroughly understood if proper attention is given to required matters
B. officer reading on post will impress unfavorably official and other visitors
C. officer should give undivided attention to the responsibilities of the post
D. only newspapers and books which relate to correctional work should be read by the officer while on duty

24. Of the following, the MAIN reason why it is very important that all eating utensils be carefully accounted for after each meal by prison inmates is that 24.____

A. accounting for such utensils should not be the responsibility of the kitchen staff alone
B. such utensils can sometimes be used as weapons by inmates
C. the steady loss of such utensils adds too much to the cost of prison operation
D. the use of such utensils is a privilege and not a right

25. Of the following, the MAIN reason why a material witness to a crime is sometimes kept in jail until the trial of the accused is over is that the 25.____

A. danger of the witness being harmed is thereby reduced
B. evidence may show that the witness is also involved in the crime
C. law requires it in all cases
D. witness will be more willing to cooperate with the District Attorney

26. From the point of view of society in general, it is MOST desirable that the diet for prison inmates be 26.____

A. as inexpensive as possible but tasty, varied, and healthy
B. of the same level as that of the person of average income outside the prison
C. the same as that for the prison administration in order to avoid food riots
D. the very minimum required to maintain life

27. In the institutions of the Department of Correction are kept not only sentenced prisoners but also accused persons awaiting trial. 27.____
Of the following, the MOST probable reason why some accused persons are kept in jail while awaiting trial is that

A. as the weight of the evidence is against the accused, they must prove their innocence
B. they have been unable to furnish the bail set by the court
C. they will be discouraged from giving false testimony at the time of the trial
D. this makes it easier for the District Attorney to prepare his case

28. Of the following, the MOST probable reason why the years between 18 and 35 have been referred to as *the age of criminality of man* is that 28.____

A. a person under 18 is classed as a juvenile delinquent while a person over 35 has established family ties which keep him from criminal activities
B. most crimes are committed by persons in that age group
C. most people are exposed to criminal influences during those years
D. these are the least stable years in the average person's life

29. Studies have shown that most crimes are committed between 9 P.M. and 12 Midnight. 29.____
Of the following, the LEAST probable reason for this is that during these hours there is a(n)

A. *decrease* in the chance of being caught
B. *increase* in business and commerce
C. *increase* in leisure time
D. *increase* in social contacts

30. Of the following, the condition that would probably lead to the GREATEST public criticism of the granting of parole to convicted offenders would be the 30.____

A. coddling of prison inmates
B. commission of crimes by parolees
C. interference by politicians in prison management
D. use of parole with second offenders

31. Of the following, the BEST evidence in support of the theory that fluctuations in the crime rate are not caused by economic conditions alone is the 31.____

A. commission of crimes against property by well-to-do people
B. decrease in crime accompanying an increase in employment opportunities
C. higher rate of unemployment among convicted persons
D. low economic status of convicted offenders

32. From time to time, there has been public criticism of the practice of providing recreational programs for prison inmates. 32.____
Such criticism is

A. *justified* because if the prison experience is made too pleasant, it will not be an effective crime preventive
B. *justified* because such programs are an unnecessary expense on the public budget
C. *unjustified* because such programs are not very expensive
D. *unjustified* because such programs help to make inmates law-abiding citizens

33. After they have served a part of their sentence, offenders are released under the continued custody of the state and under conditions that permit their reimprisonment in the event of misbehavior. 33.____
The preceding statement defines MOST accurately

A. bail B. pardon C. parole D. probation

34. The correction officer plays a very important role in the rehabilitation of the inmate for it is the correction officer who spends the most time with the inmate. 34.____
Of the following, the MOST accurate statement based on the preceding statement is that

A. a great deal of time is required to successfully rehabilitate any inmate
B. any individual who spends time with inmates can contribute a great deal to their rehabilitation
C. during the period of imprisonment, the inmate has the greatest amount of contact with the correction officer
D. most inmates go to the correction officer for guidance

35. A large proportion of persons in short-term penal institutions are there because of their inability to pay fines. 35.____
Of the following, the MOST accurate conclusion based on the preceding statement is that

A. courts sometimes impose a fine as an alternative to a jail sentence
B. law violators who are fined are kept in short-term institutions
C. many fines are for rather large amounts as shown by the inability of the fined person to pay
D. persons who are sentenced to short-term institutions may, if they do not wish to serve the sentence, pay a fine instead

36. Good discipline in a prison means an undisturbed procedure so organized that the presence of the executive head may be dispensed with from time to time. 36.___
According to the preceding statement, it is MOST reasonable to assume that

A. if prison routines are disturbed during the absence of the executive head, a breakdown in discipline is sure to result
B. in a prison where good discipline exists, occasional absences of the warden do not interfere with smooth operation
C. in a well-organized prison with an established procedure, areas and levels of responsibility are clearly defined and problems of discipline do not exist
D. the executive head of a prison is not needed if good discipline exists

37. The distinction in the criminal law of the United States between a misdemeanant and a felon was that the former received a sentence under a year whereas the latter received a sentence of a year or over. 37.___

Of the following, the MOST accurate conclusion based on the preceding statement is that under the criminal law of the United States, 37.___
A. a felony was considered a more serious crime than a misdemeanor
B. all crimes were classified as misdemeanors or felonies
C. all persons accused of felonies received sentences of more than a year
D. some misdemeanants received the same prison sentence as some felons

38. Paroles may be granted by the board of managers at any time and prisoners are referred to the board for parole consideration whenever the warden and the classification committee believe they have received the maximum benefit from institutional treatment and training and the conditions in the community are relatively favorable. 38.___
Of the following, the MOST accurate conclusion based on the preceding statement is that

A. a parole, to be valid, must be approved by the classification committee and the board of managers
B. during periods of economic depression very few paroles are granted because employment conditions in the community are not favorable
C. prisoners become eligible for parole upon completion of the required minimum part of their sentence, provided their conduct in prison has been satisfactory
D. prisoners who have not yet benefited from the institutional treatment program are not likely to be referred for parole consideration

39. No other aspect of prison life has invaded the public interest as frequently as the matter of punishment. According to the preceding statement, it is MOST reasonable to assume that the 39.___

A. extent of public interest in all prison matters is very great
B. punishment is not the only aspect of prison life that the public has been interested in
C. punishment of any prison inmate will be criticized by the public whenever it is brought to light
D. study of the punishment of prison inmates is not an easy task

40. Prison officials have been afraid of the prisoner because they saw him not as a single unit but in his aggregate aspect as the whole population of the institution. According to the preceding statement, it is MOST reasonable to assume that prison officials have been afraid of the prisoner because 40._____

A. during any prison riot every prisoner in the institution is a dangerous individual
B. each prisoner is representative of any other prisoner
C. they feared a possible attack by the individual prisoner
D. they recognized the possible danger of united action by all the prisoners

41. If a defendant in a lower court is unable to pay the fines and costs, he must usually serve time in the jail or workhouse in order to *work off* the payment at so much per day. 41._____
Of the following, the MOST valid conclusion based on the preceding statement is that the

A. greater the fine in a lower court, the longer the jail sentence that must be served in place thereof
B. money earned by inmates serving time in a jail or workhouse must be used to pay the fines and costs
C. sentences in the lower courts are only for a few days
D. sentences in the lower courts are to jail and workhouses while sentences in the higher courts are to state prisons

42. In 1997, there were 99,249 inmates confined in penal institutions operated by local jurisdictions, composed mainly of jails and workhouses, whereas there were 217,919 inmates in penal establishments operated by federal and state governments, composed mainly of prisons and reformatories. 42._____
According to the preceding statement, in 1997

A. federal and state governments did not operate jails and workhouses
B. most inmates were confined in locally operated jails, workhouses, prisons, or reformatories
C. the number of inmates in locally operated penal institutions was less than half the number in state and federally operated institutions
D. the total of more than three hundred thousand inmates confined does not include any inmates confined in local institutions which were not jails and workhouses

43. Punishment in prison is of two kinds: the infliction of pain or discomfort or the negative aspect, namely, the deprivation of normal comfort or privileges. 43._____
According to the preceding statement, it is MOST reasonable to assume that in prison the

A. deprivation of normal comfort or privileges has a negative effect
B. deprivation of privileges is a less effective form of punishment than the infliction of pain
C. infliction of pain or discomfort on a prisoner as a form of punishment brings positive results
D. taking away from a prisoner the privilege of reading mail is a form of punishment

44. A feature of present day penology is that most prisoners are eventually released to society where their success or failure will, in large measure, depend on the calibre of their intramural care and treatment and the efficiency of their parole plans and supervision. Of the following, the MOST reasonable conclusion based on the preceding statement is that 44.___

A. a former prisoner's failure to make a good adjustment after release can sometimes be due in part to a poor parole plan
B. imprisonment and parole have the same objectives
C. the main objective of present day penology is the release of prisoners back into society as soon as possible
D. with proper care, treatment, and supervision while in prison and when on parole, any convict can be successfully restored to society

45. The sentence imposed by the court on a convicted person is a poor indication of the actual time the offender will spend in prison.
In most cases, this is so MAINLY because 45.___

A. hardened criminals will make successful attempts to escape
B. the prisoner may be pardoned
C. the sentence may be reduced by the Governor on recommendation of the District Attorney
D. time off may be earned for good behavior

46. The old prison is gradually being changed into something that might diagnose and treat the prisoners rather than punish them.
According to the preceding statement, 46.___

A. diagnosis and treatment will succeed whenever punishment fails
B. the objectives and methods of the prison are being modified
C. the old prison and the new have very little in common
D. where diagnosis and treatment fail, punishment must be tried

47. Under the state-use system of prison labor, the state conducts a business of manufacture but the use or sale of the goods is limited to the institution where manufactured or to other state institutions and agencies.
According to the preceding statement, under the state-use system of prison labor, the 47.___

A. goods manufactured can be used only by state prisons
B. products of inmate labor cannot be sold on the open market
C. state competes with private industry in the manufacture of all those articles which are needed to operate a penal institution
D. variety of articles manufactured is limited to those which can be used in the institution where they are made

48. Jails and workhouses take care of an unusually large number of psychopathic and mentally abnormal individuals but the available data do not permit accurate comparisons with the distribution of mental abnormality in prisons and reformatories.
According to the preceding statement, it is MOST correct to state that 48.____

A. a conclusion on the basis of the available data that there are more or fewer psychopathic individuals in jails than in prisons is likely to be incorrect
B. a very large number of individuals of abnormal mentality are to be found in prisons and reformatories
C. the available data regarding the distribution of mentally abnormal individuals in penal institutions is inaccurate
D. the distribution of psychopathic and mentally abnormal individuals in jails and workhouses cannot be compared with the distribution of such individuals in prisons and reformatories

49. Penologists are advocating the extension of the indeterminate sentence to the misdemeanant group so that the institution can relate the inmate's progress to his release.
According to the preceding statement, it is MOST correct to say that a feature of the indeterminate sentence is that 49.____

A. an inmate who does not show satisfactory progress can be kept in jail indefinitely until he is completely rehabilitated
B. it was first used with the misdemeanant group of prisoners
C. the time to be served is at least a year but no more than two years
D. two inmates sentenced for the same class of offense do not necessarily have to serve the same amount of time

50. Adequate personnel is the first and most important ingredient of a good institutional program.
Of the following, the CHIEF justification of the preceding statement is that 50.____

A. a good institutional program cannot be developed unless the personnel required to put it into effect has first been assembled
B. many institutions do not have adequate personnel
C. the best institutional program is not likely to succeed without the personnel qualified to carry it out
D. there are several ingredients in a good personnel program

# KEY (CORRECT ANSWERS)

| | | | | | | | | | |
|---|---|---|---|---|---|---|---|---|---|
| 1. | A | 11. | B | 21. | A | 31. | A | 41. | A |
| 2. | B | 12. | A | 22. | A | 32. | D | 42. | C |
| 3. | A | 13. | A | 23. | C | 33. | C | 43. | D |
| 4. | C | 14. | A | 24. | B | 34. | C | 44. | A |
| 5. | C | 15. | B | 25. | A | 35. | A | 45. | D |
| 6. | D | 16. | C | 26. | A | 36. | B | 46. | B |
| 7. | A | 17. | D | 27. | B | 37. | A | 47. | B |
| 8. | B | 18. | D | 28. | B | 38. | D | 48. | A |
| 9. | A | 19. | B | 29. | B | 39. | B | 49. | D |
| 10. | C | 20. | D | 30. | B | 40. | D | 50. | C |

# TEST 2

DIRECTIONS: Each question or incomplete statement is followed by several suggested answers or completions. Select the one that BEST answers the question or completes the statement. *PRINT THE LETTER OF THE CORRECT ANSWER IN THE SPACE AT THE RIGHT.*

1. It is recommended that the number of cells in a new prison be determined not by the expected average population of the prison but by the expected maximum. Of the following, the BEST argument in support of the preceding recommendation is that the 1.____

   A. average population is of no value as an index of the number of prisoners who are likely to be received at an institution
   B. number of cells in a prison should be as great as possible
   C. prison should be constructed as economically as possible
   D. prison should be equipped to handle the greatest load it is likely to get

2. A crime is nothing more than behavior; it may be one act or a form of conduct which is unacceptable to the organized social group at a given time and in a given place, so unacceptable that the community has prohibited it by law. According to the preceding statement, 2.____

   A. an act that is prohibited by law is a crime
   B. behavior which is against the welfare of society is a crime
   C. conduct which is unacceptable to the community constitutes a crime
   D. unacceptable behavior and crime are the same thing

3. Parole has far less potential danger to the public than the unconditional release of an offender at the full expiration of the sentence since it permits a period of close watching with the safeguard of a possible return to the institution if the proper adjustment is not made. According to the preceding statement, it is MOST correct to state that 3.____

   A. offenders should have a short period of close watching after their release from prison
   B. paroled offenders can be returned to prison under certain conditions
   C. the advantages of parole are more numerous than its disadvantages
   D. the unconditional release of an offender is dangerous to the public

4. Full completions of the sentence means that the final limit of the penalty imposed by the court has been reached and there is no longer any legal authority over the offender in connection with that particular offense. According to the preceding statement, where there is full completion of the sentence, 4.____

   A. no further punishment or restraint can be imposed by the government for the offense in question
   B. the court has given the maximum penalty permitted under the law and society can no longer impose any legal restrictions on the offender
   C. the full limit of the penalty permitted by law for the offense has not been imposed by the court
   D. there is no longer any legal authority over the former offender

5. The ratio of male to female prisoners received in jails and workhouses is 14 to 1. Of the following, the MOST valid conclusion based on the preceding statement is that 5.____

A. female prisoners constitute one-fourteenth of all the prisoners received in jails and workhouses
B. in any group of prisoners received at a jail or workhouse it is unlikely that there will be more than one female prisoner
C. male prisoners constitute 14 percent of all prisoners received in jails and workhouses
D. on the average, for every 1400 male prisoners received in jails and workhouses, 100 female prisoners are received

6. Of the following, the MAIN reason why it is preferable to use a sterile rather than a non-sterile dressing directly over a wound is that the sterile dressing is 6.____

A. cheaper
B. easier for the first aider to make
C. easier to apply
D. less likely to contain germs

7. Suppose that an inmate has stopped breathing as the result of an accident. After sending for medical assistance, the correction officer should then immediately 7.____

A. administer a strong drink
B. begin to rub the victim's hands
C. place the victim on a bed and cover with blankets
D. start artificial respiration

8. In dealing with an external wound, the first and most important thing to do is to stop severe bleeding. Of the following, the CHIEF justification for this statement is that 8.____

A. death can result from too much loss of blood
B. external wounds are sometimes more serious than internal wounds
C. infection will set in if bleeding is not stopped
D. severe bleeding is evidence that an artery has been cut

9. A correction officer must exercise extreme care in moving an inmate who has just suffered a simple fracture MAINLY because of the danger of 9.____

A. causing additional fractures in other bones
B. increasing the bleeding
C. the broken bone pushing through the skin
D. the victim losing consciousness

10. Suppose you believe that an inmate is going to faint. Of the following, the BEST first aid measure for you to take FIRST is to 10.____

A. have the inmate walk up and back briskly
B. lay the inmate down, head level with or lower than the rest of the body
C. rub the inmate's hands and arms vigorously
D. seat the inmate erect in a chair and offer some water or other liquid to drink

11. We should beware of assuming that a new jail necessarily means a good penal institution. 11.____
This statement implies MOST directly that

A. not all good penal institutions are new
B. not all old jails are bad penal institutions
C. some new jails are not good penal institutions
D. some old jails are good penal institutions

12. A good probation department, by furnishing the judge with information regarding the guilty individual, makes possible discrimination in the use of imprisonment and, in the person of the probation officer, provides a substitute for it. 12.____
Of the following, the MOST direct implication of the preceding statement is that

A. a properly functioning probation department offers the means for effective use of probation in lieu of imprisonment for some offenders
B. if used with discrimination by the judge, probation is sometimes in itself an indirect form of punishment
C. probation, as a substitute for imprisonment, should be more widely used
D. the primary function of a good probation officer is to secure background information about the offender

13. The fact that the offense is not serious does not mean that the perpetrator can be easily turned into a law-abiding citizen. 13.____
Of the following, the BEST evidence in support of this statement is the

A. high rate of recidivism among misdemeanant prisoners
B. large number of small jails
C. number of prisoners who violate parole
D. reluctance of society to accept the former convict

14. The chain of prison administration is only as strong as its weakest officer. 14.____
The preceding statement implies MOST directly that

A. careful selection and proper training of personnel are not sufficiently emphasized by many prison administrators
B. every prison employee is basically an administrator
C. one inefficient officer can sometimes seriously impair the functioning of an entire institution
D. the chainlike organization of prison management becomes apparent when a weak officer fails to perform his job properly

15. The industrial farm is the best type of institution yet developed for the majority of jail prisoners. 15.____
Of the following, the BEST justification for this statement is that in an institution of this type

A. strictest application of advanced classification procedure is possible
B. the products of inmate labor in large measure pay for the cost of running the institution

C. there is likely to be freedom from political interference because it is located away from urban centers
D. worthwhile employment and training in desirable surroundings can be afforded every inmate

16. Several studies have shown that the majority of sentenced workhouse prisoners are recidivists. 16.____
Of the following, the MOST valid inference based on the preceding statement is that

A. commitment procedures for certain classes of prisoners should be re-studied
B. for many prisoners custody, rather than rehabilitation, should be emphasized
C. the rate of recidivism is greatest among workhouse prisoners
D. while prison administrators give more attention to rehabilitative measures today, results are generally poor

17. It is desirable that the prisoners be well-acquainted with the practices and procedures of the parole board. Of the following, the BEST argument in favor of this policy is that 17.____

A. parole practices and procedures often change with a change in the make-up of the parole board
B. prisoner participation in the formulation of parole board practices and procedures is desirable
C. prisoners will be less prone to think they were unjustly treated by the parole board
D. the parole board will be less subject to public criticism

18. Of the following, the MOST probable reason why public criticism of recreational programs for prisoners is much less common today than it was twenty-five years ago is that the general public nowadays 18.____

A. accepts the rehabilitative objectives of correctional institutions more readily
B. comprehends the real value of recreation in the correctional program
C. is more interested in recreation and sports
D. understands the problems involved in the maintenance of prison discipline

19. Of the following, the CHIEF value of the indeterminate sentence is that 19.____

A. better discipline is obtained from the prisoner during the period of his incarceration
B. the length of time to be served can be adjusted to the seriousness of the crime
C. the sentencing power of the courts is curtailed
D. the time spent in jail can be related to the rate of rehabilitative progress

20. Suppose that a study of prison inmates shows that a relatively small percentage of first offenders become second offenders, but that a very large percentage of second offenders commit subsequent offenses. 20.____
Of the following, the LEAST valid inference based on the study described is that

A. correctional procedures presently employed with second offenders are largely ineffective
B. first offenders offer the most fertile field for rehabilitative efforts
C. in a random sampling of prisoners, most of those sampled will have committed two or more offenses
D. it is more difficult to attain success in the rehabilitation of second offenders than in the rehabilitation of first offenders

21. Progressive penologists GENERALLY are of the opinion that 21.____

A. alcoholics should be sentenced to jail for at least six months so that a cure can be effected
B. alcoholics should receive an indeterminate rather than a definite jail term
C. chronic alcoholism is a sickness rather than a crime
D. treatment for chronic alcoholism should be made compulsory

22. It has been proposed that wider use be made of fines in lieu of imprisonment as a method of punishment for certain offenses. 22.____
Of the following, the BEST argument in support of this proposal is that

A. contact with prison atmosphere is often an effective deterrent to a repetition of the offense
B. fines are not difficult to collect
C. fines can be adjusted to the ability of the offender to pay
D. imprisonment is expensive for the government

23. Penologists are generally opposed to the use of force as a method of maintaining prison discipline MAINLY because 23.____

A. it is difficult to limit its use to self-defense or the enforcement of lawful commands
B. it is of doubtful legality
C. modern escape-proof institutions have reduced the discipline problem to a minimum
D. resentment of the use of force by inmates may create, rather than correct, discipline problems

24. Of the following, the MAIN reason why it is so difficult to eradicate the smuggling of narcotics into a prison is that 24.____

A. it is not possible to measure the personal integrity of prison personnel prior to their appointment to the service
B. so many prison inmates are drug addicts today
C. there are so many possible ways for the drugs to enter the prison
D. the supply of available drugs is constantly increasing

25. Of the following, the LEAST valid argument in favor of having a commissary in a correctional institution is that the commissary 25.____

A. contributes to the maintenance of inmate morale
B. helps to reduce the institution's food budget
C. is an important aid in maintaining discipline
D. provides funds, not otherwise available, to buy recreational equipment for inmates

26. Of the following, the CHIEF argument in favor of dormitories over cells as a method of housing prison inmates is that dormitories 26.____

A. are cheaper to construct
B. are easier to clean
C. make custodial supervision easier
D. are preferred by inmates

27. In comparing the Pennsylvania with the Auburn system of penal discipline, it is MOST correct to state that in the 27.____

A. Auburn system the prisoners were completely separated from each other except at meal time
B. Auburn system the prisoners were not permitted to talk to each other
C. Pennsylvania system prison visiting was prohibited
D. Pennsylvania system the prisoners were allowed to mingle with each other only when at work

28. The proper Fahrenheit temperature which should be maintained in a cell block during the winter months is MOST NEARLY 28.____

A. $60^{\circ}$ B. $65^{\circ}$ C. $73^{\circ}$ D. $75^{\circ}$

29. In the ten years from 1970 to 1980, in the nation as a whole, the 29.____

A. number of major crimes remained constant but the number of lesser offenses increased markedly
B. percentage increase in population was greater than the percentage increase in major crimes
C. percentage increase in population was smaller than the percentage increase in major crimes
D. percentage increase in population equaled the percentage increase in major crimes

Questions 30-34.

DIRECTIONS: For each book in Column I below, select the author of the book from Column II; then write the letter preceding the author's name in the space at the right.

| COLUMN I | COLUMN II | |
|---|---|---|
| 30. JAILS - CARE AND TREATMENT OF MISDEMEANANT PRISONERS IN THE UNITED STATES | A. Barnes, Harry E., and Teeters, Negley, K. | 30.____ |
| | B. Glueck, Sheldon and Eleanor | |
| 31. NEW HORIZONS IN CRIMINOLOGY | C. Harris, Mary B. | 31.____ |
| 32. PROBATION AND PAROLE | D. Monahan, Florence | 32.____ |
| 33. THE TRAINING OF PRISON GUARDS IN THE STATE OF NEW YORK | E. Pigeon, Helen D. | 33.____ |
| 34. WOMEN IN CRIME | F. Robinson, Louis N. | 34.____ |
| | G. Wallack, Walter M. | |

35. A person with a *psychopathic personality* is 35.____

A. consistently abnormal in his behavior B. feebleminded
C. insane and has criminal tendencies D. psychotic

36. A person is considered to be of normal intelligence if his IQ or intelligence quotient falls within the range of 36.____

A. 60-80 B. 70-90 C. 80-100 D. 90-110

37. The term *malingerer* is MOST correctly applied to an inmate who 37.____

A. bears an officer a grudge for a long time
B. is a habitual liar
C. pretends to be ill in order to avoid working
D. takes a long time to recover from an illness

38. Members of the uniformed force of the City Department of Correction are designated as peace officers by the 38.____

A. Administrative Code
B. City Charter
C. Code of Criminal Procedure
D. Penal Law

39. According to the Penal Law, escape from lawful imprisonment in this state is ALWAYS a 39.____

A. felony
B. felony if the imprisonment was for a felony
C. misdemeanor
D. misdemeanor if the imprisonment was for a felony

40. A writ or order by a magistrate, justice, or other competent authority and addressed to an officer requiring him to arrest the person named therein and bring him before the court to be examined regarding the offense with which he is charged.
The preceding definition refers MOST directly to a 40.____

A. certificate of reasonable doubt
B. mandamus
C. warrant
D. writ of habeas corpus

41. The MOST accurate of the following statements about the offenses for which prisoners were sentenced to the institutions of the Department last year is that the 41.____

A. largest number of male commitments was for disorderly conduct whereas the largest number of female commitments was for vagrancy (prostitution)
B. largest number of male commitments was for vagrancy whereas the largest number of female commitments was for disorderly conduct
C. number of women committed for drug offenses was about 50% of the number of men committed for drug offenses
D. second largest number of male commitments was for gambling whereas the second largest number of female commitments was for petit larceny

42. Of the inmates committed to the Department last year, the average age of the inmates committed to the workhouse as compared to the average age of the inmates committed to the penitentiary was 42.____

A. higher
B. higher for male commitments but lower for female commitments
C. lower
D. neither higher nor lower

43. Of all the inmates sentenced to the institutions of the Department last year, those who had any education beyond the elementary school constituted between 43.____

A. 15% and 20%
B. 10% and 15%
C. 5% and 10%
D. 0% and 5%

44. Last year the average rate of recidivism among workhouse and penitentiary inmates (men and women) in the institutions of the Department was 44.____

A. between 50% and 60%
B. less than 30%
C. more than 30%, but less than 55%
D. more than 60%, but less than 75%

45. In the detention prisons of the Department, persons charged with felonies GENERALLY constitute 45.____

A. about half of the inmate population
B. a majority of the inmate population
C. a minority of the inmate population
D. less of a discipline problem than persons charged with misdemeanors

46. It is important that the tier officer be notified as soon as possible of any change in an inmate's court status MAINLY because 46.____

A. a change in an inmate's court status may necessitate a change in custodial supervision
B. prison records to be of value must be accurate and up-to-date
C. subordinates should not be able to justify errors of judgment on the grounds of ignorance of the facts
D. the tier officer, who supervises many inmates, may find it difficult to remember every detail of each inmate's status

47. The LEAST accurate of the following statements is that a 47.____

A. commitment under an alternate sentence of a fine or a definite term can be made both to the workhouse and to the penitentiary
B. maximum workhouse definite sentence is for a longer period than a maximum penitentiary definite sentence
C. maximum workhouse indefinite sentence is for a shorter period than a maximum penitentiary indefinite sentence
D. minimum penitentiary definite sentence is for a longer period than a minimum workhouse definite sentence

48. A *short commitment* is a commitment issued by a magistrate wherein the defendant is 48.____

A. held for future action in the Magistrates Courts
B. held for the Court of Special Sessions
C. held for the Grand Jury
D. sentenced by the magistrate for the offense committed

49. When the arresting officer calls for an inmate to produce the inmate in court to answer to the charge, it is important that he be informed by the pen officer of any warrants against the inmate MAINLY because 49.____

A. it may be necessary to produce the warrants in court together with the inmate
B. the inmate may be released on the original charge
C. the warrants may be for more serious offenses than the present arrest
D. this information will help to identify the inmate

50. When a prisoner is committed on a direct admission, the officer at the detention pen is required to note on the back of the commitment the condition of the inmate at the time when taken into custody by the Department. 50.____
Of the following, the PRINCIPAL reason why this information is important is that

A. a comparison can be made at the time of release to see if any improvement has been made
B. drug addicts and alcoholics can be noted and segregated
C. it may influence the determination as to which institution the inmate is to be transferred
D. subsequent charges that an inmate was mistreated while in the Department's custody can be refuted

# KEY (CORRECT ANSWERS)

| | | | | |
|---|---|---|---|---|
| 1. D | 11. C | 21. C | 31. A | 41. A |
| 2. A | 12. A | 22. D | 32. E | 42. A |
| 3. B | 13. A | 23. D | 33. G | 43. D |
| 4. A | 14. C | 24. C | 34. D | 44. C |
| 5. D | 15. D | 25. B | 35. A | 45. B |
| 6. D | 16. A | 26. A | 36. D | 46. A |
| 7. D | 17. C | 27. B | 37. C | 47. B |
| 8. A | 18. A | 28. B | 38. C | 48. A |
| 9. C | 19. D | 29. C | 39. B | 49. B |
| 10. B | 20. C | 30. F | 40. C | 50. D |

# EXAMINATION SECTION
# TEST 1

DIRECTIONS: Each question or incomplete statement is followed by several suggested answers or completions. Select the one that BEST answers the question or completes the statement. *PRINT THE LETTER OF THE CORRECT ANSWER IN THE SPACE AT THE RIGHT.*

1. The shift from an individual to a formal response of crime resulted in which one of the following: 1.____

   A. Elimination of revenge
   B. Made punishment more humane
   C. Lessened the chances of longstanding family feuds
   D. Promoted citizen disinterest in crime and the punishment of criminals
   E. Contributed to the development of a more just method of determining guilt

2. The MOST important trend in corrections today: 2.____

   A. Attempt to reinforce any ties between the offender and the community
   B. Long sentences
   C. Less use of confinement if possible
   D. Developing programs for prisoners in prisons
   E. None of the above

3. People commit crimes because 3.____

   A. they are mentally ill
   B. they come from poor families
   C. it is their way of trying to solve their problems
   D. they want to
   E. they are born criminals

4. The jail officer's role in the jail is to 4.____

   I. represent the sheriff
   II. represent the criminal justice system
   III. assume responsibility for the welfare of prisoners
   IV. punish prisoners for their crimes
   V. appease social pressure

   The CORRECT answer is:

   A. I, II    B. II, III    C. I, II, III
   D. II, III, IV    E. II, V

5. Which one of the following is a *genuine* characteristic of a professional jail officer? He 5.____

   A. becomes easily upset by prisoners
   B. wants to punish prisoners for their crimes
   C. tries to treat all prisoners alike without favoritism or emotion
   D. refuses to discuss the prisoners' guilt or innocence
   E. is critical of the courts and the law and says so to prisoners

# KEY (CORRECT ANSWERS)

1. E
2. A
3. C
4. B
5. C

# TEST 2

DIRECTIONS: Each question or incomplete statement is followed by several suggested answers or completions. Select the one that BEST answers the question or completes the statement. *PRINT THE LETTER OF THE CORRECT ANSWER IN THE SPACE AT THE RIGHT.*

1. From the list below, select the one that is legally proper on which the jail officer can book a prisoner: 1.____

   A. Larceny
   B. Hold for Dr. Jones
   C. False identification
   D. Suspicion
   E. Hold for investigation

2. The purpose of a strip search is: 2.____
   I. To discover contraband
   II. To let the prisoner know that he is now in jail
   III. To discover if he has lice
   IV. To appraise physical condition
   V. All of the above

   The CORRECT answer is:

   A. I, II
   B. II, III
   C. I, IV
   D. I, III
   E. V

3. Select those statements that are TRUE about strip and frisk searches: 3.____
   I. If you are not certain that you examined an area, return to it
   II. All searches should be systematic
   III. An incomplete search is as bad as no search at all
   IV. Your attitude when conducting the search is as important as the way the search is done
   V. All of the above

   The CORRECT answer is:

   A. I, III
   B. II, III
   C. II, III, IV
   D. I, III, IV
   E. V

4. Identification procedures are important because: 4.____
   I. The FBI requires them
   II. It is a method of identifying those persons who are wanted by other jurisdictions
   III. It is a method of identifying prisoners when they are released
   IV. It is necessary for statistical purposes
   V. All of the above

   The CORRECT answer is:

   A. II, III
   B. I, IV
   C. II, IV
   D. I, II
   E. V

5. Physical examinations for all prisoners at the time of admission are 5.____

   A. a waste of time since most of them are drunks anyway
   B. necessary to discover the sick and injured
   C. necessary only if a prisoner seems to be obviously sick
   D. duplicatory of previous physicals

6. Which of the following are NOT accurate descriptions of personal property and should not be used? 6.____

   I. Gold watch
   II. Plaid sport coat, size 40
   III. Yellow metal ring with diamond
   IV. Brown suit, Bonds label, hole in left elbow, trousers soiled at right knee, size 40
   V. Timex watch

   The CORRECT answer is:

   A. I, II, V
   B. II, III, V
   C. I, IV, V
   D. I, II, III
   E. I, III, V

7. Bathing of all prisoners when they are admitted to the jail is necessary for the following reasons: 7.____

   I. It is good for staff morale to see clean prisoners
   II. Prevent vermin from entering the jail
   III. No one likes dirty people
   IV. It contributes to the health and well-being of prisoners
   V. All of the above

   The CORRECT answer is:

   A. I, II
   B. II, III
   C. III, IV
   D. II, IV
   E. V

8. Prisoners should not be permitted to wear long hair because 8.____

   A. it is unsightly
   B. it is unsanitary
   C. the jail staff do not like it
   D. all of the above
   E. none of the above

9. All prisoners should wear jail clothing because 9.____

   A. they look neater when they all are dressed alike
   B. it is a good security procedure since it makes escape difficult
   C. it is simpler for them to do their laundry
   D. it is cheaper

10. Match the following descriptions of prisoners with the appropriate housing assignment: 10.

   A. Juvenile prisoner A.____
   B. Elderly or infirm prisoner B.____
   C. Mentally ill prisoner C.____
   D. Hostile aggressive prisoner D.____

   1. dormitory, near infirmary
   2. in single cell away from all adults
   3. in a single cell
   4. in a single cell under close supervision
   5. in a padded cell

11. The PROPER definition of contraband is: 11.____

A. Any item that can be used as a weapon, and all drugs
B. All items listed as contraband and posted in the jail
C. All items not issued by the jail and not specifically authorized
D. Illicit guns.

12. Cell searches are necessary for the following reason: 12.____

A. To discover contraband
B. To keep prisoners off balance
C. To reduce clutter
D. All of the above

13. Identify the two MOST important principles of a cell search: 13.____

I. Examine everything in the cell
II. Be systematic
III. Leave the cell in the same condition in which it was found
IV. Ignore the prisoner when searching his cell
V. Remain aloof

The CORRECT answer is:

A. I, II
B. II, III
C. III, IV
D. IV, V
E. I, III

14. Indicate whether the following statements are TRUE or FALSE: 14.

A. Counts are unnecessary if prisoners are locked up at all times. A.____
B. A jail officer should know how many prisoners he has at all times. B.____
C. One officer can make an accurate count in a dormitory. C.____
D. Roll call counts are easy to take and make good sense. D.____
E. When counting prisoners, the officer must always see flesh. E.____
F. It is not good practice to permit prisoners to conduct a count F.____

15. Select the statements that are examples of good key control: 15.____

I. Since minimum security prisoners can be trusted, it is proper to permit them to use keys to unlock and lock all doors
II. A jail officer should never carry both inside and outside keys
III. Jail officers should be permitted to exchange keys during shift change
IV. All security keys should be concealed when carried
V. None of the above

The CORRECT answer is:

A. I, III
B. II, III
C. II, IV
D. I, IV
E. V

16. The single MOST effective security measure in the jail is 16.____

A. remote TV camera
B. tool-hardened steel
C. metal detectors
D. the alertness of the jail officer
E. stoolies

17. Indicate whether the following statements are TRUE or FALSE: 17.

A. Weapons are needed in the jail in order to protect personnel A.____
B. Gas in aerosol cans and clubs are not weapons B.____
C. The weapon carried in the jail by the officer can be taken away and used against him C.____
D. Although all jail personnel should be required to check their weapons before entering the jail, FBI agents and visiting sheriffs are exempt D.____
E. The armory should be inside the jail so that weapons will be available to jail officers when they need them E.____

---

# KEY (CORRECT ANSWERS)

1. A
2. D
3. C
4. A
5. B

6. E
7. D
8. E
9. B
10. A. 2
    B. 1
    C. 4
    D. 3

11. C
12. A
13. B
14. A. F
    B. T
    C. F
    D. F
    E. T
    F. T
15. C

16. D
17. A. F
    B. F
    C. T
    D. F
    E. F

# TEST 3

DIRECTIONS: Each question or incomplete statement is followed by several suggested answers or completions. Select the one that BEST answers the question or completes the statement. *PRINT THE LETTER OF THE CORRECT ANSWER IN THE SPACE AT THE RIGHT.*

1. What are the two MOST important changes that occur when a prisoner is admitted to the jail? He 1.____

   A. becomes a prisoner
   B. changes status from citizen to prisoner
   C. has to wear jail clothing
   D. begins to lose his identity

2. List the *tangible* items that contribute to a prisoner's identity and that are taken from him when he enters the jail. (List six.) 2.____

   1. ____________ 2. ____________
   3. ____________ 4. ____________
   5. ____________ 6. ____________

3. List the *intangibles* that contribute to a prisoner's identity that he loses when he enters the jail. (List three.) 3.____

   1. ____________ 2. ____________ 3. ____________

4. Indicate whether the following statements are TRUE or FALSE: 4.

   A. Prisoners are generally not frustrated by their inability to do things for themselves because they have few things bothering them. A.____
   B. Giving a prisoner good conduct time is equal to rewards he would receive in the community such as pay, approval, and responsibility. B.____
   C. Cutting a prisoner's hair at admission does not alter his identity. C.____
   D. A prisoner's sudden dependence on his wife and friends does not change his relationship with them. D.____
   E. There is no similarity between the feelings a prisoner has when confined and the person who is entering military service. E.____

5. The newly admitted prisoner can be assisted in adjusting to the jail by one of the following methods: 5.____

   A. Orientation by other prisoners
   B. Written rules and regulations that are given to him
   C. Trial and error and by watching others
   D. Kept in a cell until he learns jail routine

6. Although any period in confinement can be considered a critical time, the following times are especially sensitive: (Select two.) 6.____

   A. During discharge of the prisoner from the jail
   B. During searches of cells
   C. During strip or frisk searches
   D. Immediately before or after court appearances
   E. During mealtimes
   F. All of the above

7. What should be done about a prisoner who appears hostile during admission? 7.____

A. Lock him up in a cell immediately
B. Insist on carrying out the admission procedure and ask the arresting officer to assist you
C. Be certain to get all the details of the arrest and the prisoner's behavior from the arresting officer. This should be done in the presence of the prisoner so that he knows he can't fool you.
D. Get rid of the arresting officer as soon as possible. Carry out the admission procedure calmly and quietly.

8. The BEST procedure to follow when a prisoner is upset from a visit from his wife or girlfriend is to do the following: 8.____

A. Lock him in a cell by himself so that he will not try to escape and where he will not disturb others
B. Permit him to call his wife or girlfriend and correct the misunderstanding
C. Talk to the prisoner or at least be a sympathetic and understanding listener
D. If he is continuously having problems because of argument with visitors, refuse to let further visits to take place

9. Although many factors are involved in setting and controlling the jail climate, the MOST important is: 9.____

A. The behavior of the prisoners since they can be hostile and manipulative
B. The attitude and behavior of the staff
C. The quality of the food
D. Relaxed security procedures
E. All of the above

10. The following technique is useful in avoiding prisoner manipulation: 10.____

A. Refuse to discuss any prisoner's problems with him
B. Establish good communications with other staff members
C. Keep good records
D. Ignore prisoner complaints and refuse to permit any exceptions to jail rules

11. Indicate whether the following statements are TRUE or FALSE: 11.

A. A suicide attempt is usually an attempt to manipulate jail staff A.____
B. Overreacting to prisoners is an indication that the jail officer is conscientious and concerned B.____
C. A jail officer should always act knowledgeable about jail procedures even when he is not C.____
D. Jail rules seldom need to be changed; they do need to be updated by adding new rules from time to time D.____
E. There is nothing wrong with rules made up by prisoners because usually they are tougher than rules developed by the administrator E.____

12. A jail officer who overreacts to prisoners is — 12.____

 A. alert to prisoner manipulation
 B. demonstrating an interest in his work
 C. lacks confidence and is insecure
 D. all of the above

13. List characteristics of the trained, professional jailer: (List seven.) — 13.____

 1. ____________ 2. ____________
 3. ____________ 4. ____________
 5. ____________ 6. ____________
 7. ____________

14. Indicate whether the following statements are TRUE or FALSE: — 14.

 A. A jail officer who disagrees with a jail rule and lets prisoners know it will be considered an honest officer and will be contributing to a positive jail climate — A.____
 B. The jail officer who gossips with prisoners gets their respect because he is demonstrating that he is just like they are — B.____
 C. Discussing dissatisfactions about the jail with prisoners is a good way to get good suggestions for changes in jail policy — C.____
 D. Prisoners are quick to interpret differences of opinion between staff members as signs of disunity — D.____
 E. Regulations assist prisoners in adjusting to the jail by eliminating confusion — E.____
 F. Rigid rules are the most effective way of keeping order and contribute to a well-run jail and few disciplinary reports — F.____
 G. Vague regulations are an indication to prisoners that personnel do not have clear understanding or control of the jail — G.____
 H. Reasonable rules reduce staff-prisoner conflict — H.____

# KEY (CORRECT ANSWERS)

1. B, D
2. Street clothing, haircut, jewelry, belt, tie clip, cigarette lighter
3. Work, relations with his family, daily habits
4. A. F
   B. F
   C. F
   D. F
   E. F
5. B
6. C, D
7. D
8. C
9. B
10. B
11. A. F
    B. F
    C. F
    D. F
    E. F
12. C
13. Flexibility, self-confidence, willingness to make decisions, impartiality, refusal to respond in a hostile manner to prisoner hostility, respect for himself and his work, willingness to perform all necessary tasks
14. A. F
    B. F
    C. F
    D. T
    E. T
    F. F
    G. T
    H. T

# TEST 4

DIRECTIONS: Each question or incomplete statement is followed by several suggested answers or completions. Select the one that BEST answers the question or completes the statement. *PRINT THE LETTER OF THE CORRECT ANSWER IN THE SPACE AT THE RIGHT.*

1. Select the one statement that completes the following sentence. 1.____
The overall objective of supervision is

   A. achievement of security
   B. protection of prisoners
   C. teaching prisoners how to work
   D. the development of an orderly environment

2. Another important goal of supervision is control. This means: 2.____

   A. Making certain that each prisoner is either locked in his cell or under the direct physical control of the jail officer
   B. That jail officers closely supervise prisoner activities, especially where trusties are in charge of other prisoners
   C. That jail personnel supervise all prisoners, develop procedures, set standards, and evaluate results
   D. All of the above

3. An officer is placed on a new assignment where he will be supervising prisoners. 3.____
Which of the following is the proper FIRST step he should take in assuming this assignment?

   A. Call the prisoners together and tell them what kind of work he expects from them.
   B. Ask the prisoners for suggestions on how this particular operation can be improved.
   C. Ask each prisoner for a description of his work so that he can seek ways to revise procedures and make them more effective.
   D. Read post orders, familiarize himself with policies and procedures, and learn all he can about the assignment.

4. Officer P assigned four prisoners to a small empty cell block and gave them the following instructions. *I want this place cleaned up. I'll be back before the end of the day to check on your work.* 4.____
List the errors made by Officer P. (List three.)

   1. ____________________
   2. ____________________
   3. ____________________

5. A supervisor is responsible for making an accurate and honest evaluation of a prisoner's performance. 5.____
In order to do this, he must

   A. know a great deal about the prisoner, including his offense, his family life, and his education
   B. have supervised him long enough to know him well

C. recognize and account for individual differences
D. evaluate all prisoners as working equally hard or satisfactorily
E. recognize either improvement or a change for the worse and, if possible, explain it

6. Select the two statements that demonstrate a supervisor's objectivity in evaluating a prisoner: 6.____

A. This man is lazy
B. This man is always at the end of the line when picking up tools and first in line when turning them in
C. Prisoner J is one of the slowest moving men in the crew
D. Prisoner A is hard working, energetic, and always on the go
E. Prisoner S listens carefully, asks questions when he does not understand, and makes few mistakes

7. Officer R is trying hard to do a good job. He feels that it is important for jail officers to communicate with prisoners. In this way, he can keep in touch with them and their problems and, as a result, will be a more effective supervisor. This morning he came in and in talking to some of the prisoners commented that he certainly was tired; he should not have stayed out so late. Not only was he tired, but his wife was angry with him because of the late hours he keeps when bowling. 7.____
One of the prisoners asked him about his score. He replied that he averaged 105. One of the prisoners commented that this was a lady's score, and the other prisoners laughed.
What errors did Officer R make? (List three.)

1. ______________________________
2. ______________________________
3. ______________________________

8. Officer S has been talking to Prisoner O. During the conversation, O says, *"Don't you think that Idiot T would know better than to loan I cigarettes when he knows I is leaving before commissary day?"* Officer S replied, *"I never did think T had too many brains and now I'm certain of it. But then, I doesn't have too many smarts either."* What do you think Prisoner O is thinking of Officer S's remarks? (Select one.) 8.____

A. Well, we seem to agree about some things.
B. Gee, Officer S is pretty sharp about who is smart or dumb.
C. I wonder what he says about me to other prisoners.
D. He is right about T but I think I is a smart old bird. But I'm not going to argue with him.

9. Prisoner B is having problems with his wife. She wants to have their eight-year-old boy's tonsils removed, and B wants her to wait until he is released. He is discussing the problem with Officer R who tells him, *"Listen, "let her have them removed. The sooner the better; it's like pulling a tooth, fast and simple."* 9.____
Do you think this advice was good or bad? (Select one.)

A. *Good;* it will keep the wife occupied while Prisoner B is in jail.
B. *Good;* the boy should have his tonsils removed.
C. *Bad;* Officer R knows nothing about the family situation or the boy's medical condition.

D. *Bad;* he is taking the wife's side in the argument.
E. *Good;* he is giving the prisoner advice, and the prisoner needs it if he is to resolve his problem.

10. The Lockmeup County Jail is run simply and with little fuss or bother. The sheriff has found that the prisoners can pretty well take care of themselves. The jail is fairly clean and seems to be quite orderly. It seems, however, that some prisoners never do any work and always have money, cigarettes, and commissary. 10.____
What is going on here?

A. The prisoners are probably a well-behaved, cooperative group who are interested in getting along with the sheriff.
B. It is highly probable that prisoners are running the jail and have established a sanitary court.
C. Both of the above
D. None of the above

11. Officer J has assigned three prisoners to the kitchen detail to wash pots, mop the floor, and wipe tables. He will not be available to supervise them at all times. He has, therefore, given one of the prisoners responsibility for organizing the work and giving out assignments. 11.____
Is Officer J making any supervisory errors?

A. *No;* a good supervisor learns to delegate responsibility.
B. *Yes;* prisoners should never have any supervisory responsibility over other prisoners.
C. *No;* he will be checking them from time to time so there is little chance that anything will go wrong.
D. *Yes;* he has not been clear in his assignment of work.

12. Officer P is responsible for the supervision of a cell block during the evening hours when there is little activity in the jail. His post is at the door to the cell block, but he makes it a habit to make rounds of the cell block once every hour. His tour always takes place during the last 15 minutes of the hour. Officer P believes in being systematic and organized. This evening Prisoner S asked him for a light and engaged him in conversation. S is usually not talkative. The other prisoners lounging in the bullpen area between cells seemed somewhat noisier than usual, but not to the point where it would be disturbing. 12.____
What do you think could be happening in the cell block?

A. Nothing; it is not unusual for prisoners to change and become friendly. In fact, S's desire to talk should be encouraged; perhaps in time he may want to discuss his problems with Officer P.
B. An escape is in progress, and the prisoners are trying to provide a distraction.
C. These distractions could cover an escape attempt or sexual assaults in another part of the jail.
D. Nothing; the prisoner usually becomes a little noisy as the evening progresses.

13. Referring to Question 12 above, do you think Officer P is making any errors? 13.____

A. *No;* he is responding to a prisoner's need to talk to someone.
B. *Yes;* he should not make his tours through the cell block according to such a rigid schedule.

C. *No*; he seems to be alert and is actively supervising the cell block.
D. *Yes;* he should not be giving S a light.

14. The television set for prisoners is located in the day-room. Although it had been possible to buy the set with remote controls, this was not done. 14.____
How do you think the jail staff can ensure that they will exercise control over the set?
    I. The threat of losing the television will be enough to keep the prisoners in line.
    II. The on-off switch should be controlled by the jail staff.
    III. The prisoners should be permitted to set up a committee to develop rules for television use.
    IV. Jail staff should set viewing hours and have the final approval over programs.

The CORRECT answer is:

A. I, II  B. II, III  C. I, IV
D. III, IV  E. II, IV

15. The jail is switching over to dining room feeding. This has been made possible by the addition of eight jail officers. 15.____
Where should the posts be located to cover the trouble spots?

A. Along the walls of the dining room
B. Circulating in the dining room
C. One watching the line entering the dining room, one in the kitchen, and the other circulating
D. One at the line entering the dining room, one at the serving line, one at the silverware collection and tray scraping can, and three either along the wall or circulating

16. List the important points in supervising the feeding of prisoners in their cells. (List four.) 16.____

1. ____________________
2. ____________________
3. ____________________
4. ____________________

17. Although the jail has a routine procedure for handling sick call, Officer P has worked out a much simpler system. Whenever a prisoner requests to see the doctor, Officer P questions him; and if the prisoner complains of a headache or cold, he is given two aspirin. This has reduced the sick call line substantially. Officer P prides himself in his ability to handle sick call requests and to spot the chronic complainers. 17.____
Do you feel that Officer P's behavior is proper?
    I. No; jail officers should not give out medication.
    II. Yes; doctors are busy and reducing the number of sick call requests will help them give more time to those who are really sick.
    III. No; Officer P is diagnosing prisoner medical complaints, and he is not qualified to do this.
    IV. Yes, as long as he limits his medical activity to those who have colds and headaches.
    V. Yes; after all, the prisoners are diagnosing their condition by telling Officer P that they have colds or headaches. Furthermore, aspirin is not medicine.

The CORRECT answer is:

A. I, III  B. I, II  C. III, IV
D. I, IV  E. III, V

18. List the five BASIC principles of supervising prisoners on sick call and during their medical care. 18.____

1. ______________________
2. ______________________
3. ______________________
4. ______________________
5. ______________________

19. Supervising visiting is a dull assignment to Officer K. He manages to pass the time by concentrating on the visiting couple who are seated nearest him. Usually, he overhears some interesting conversations. Visiting in this jail is done in a room with tables that have a four-inch partition running through their center. Today, Officer K became so interested in the visit of the prisoner and his girlfriend seated near him that he didn't realize that he was permitting them and other prisoners to visit longer than regulations allowed. 19.____
Do you think Officer K has made any errors?
I. No; he was giving close supervision to the visitors.
II. Yes; it is not his responsibility to eavesdrop on visitors' conversations.
III. No; permitting visiting to last longer than regulations allow is not an error.
IV. Yes; he was distracted by one visitor and did not pay any attention to other visiting taking place.
The CORRECT answer is:

A. III, IV
B. III, V
C. II, IV
D. I, II
E. II, III

20. Which of the following descriptive statements are included in a definition of a trusty. A trusty 20.____

A. is a prisoner who can be trusted to work without supervision
B. is a prisoner who can work under minimum supervision
C. can be depended on not to escape
D. is a prisoner who because he can be trusted can be given responsibility to supervise the work of other prisoners and lock and unlock cells. He thus makes the work of jail personnel much easier.

21. What *special* privileges should trusties have that are NOT permitted to other prisoners? 21.____

A. Freedom to move about in the jail without special permission
B. Extra food because they work
C. Permitted to run errands for jail personnel
D. They should not have any special privileges

22. A prisoner being considered for trusty status should be evaluated in three areas. Indicate by writing in the kinds of information that should be examined. (List three kinds.) 22.____

1. ______________________
2. ______________________
3. ______________________

23. Why must juveniles be kept separate from adult prisoners? (List two reasons.) 23.____

1. ____________________
2. ____________________

24. In what way is supervision of women DIFFERENT from supervision for men? 24.____

____________________
____________________
____________________
____________________

25. Officer W has been supervising the recreation periods recently. Yesterday, he overruled the umpire's decision even though there had been no argument from either team. There was little doubt that the umpire had made a bad call. Today, he took part in a volleyball game in order to even sides. 25.____
Do you feel Officer W has made any errors?

A. *No;* he is correcting the umpire and thus avoiding complaints or arguments from prisoners.
B. *Yes;* it seems that the prisoner did not contest the call.
C. *Yes;* he is becoming involved with prisoner recreation activities when there is no need to do so, and he is ignoring his supervisory responsibility.
D. *No;* a supervisor should be alert to possible problems and try and solve them before they become serious. Correcting the umpire was correct. He is also contributing to the recreation period by participating in the game.

26. List the BASIC principles of supervising a prisoner at a funeral or other social activity outside the jail. (List three.) 26.____

1. ____________________
2. ____________________
3. ____________________

# KEY (CORRECT ANSWERS)

1. D
2. C
3. D
4. Poor directions - too general; did not take into account the possibility that some of the prisoners may not have understood his orders; is not making periodic cheeks.
5. C
6. B, E
7. A. Discussed his off-duty activities with prisoners.
   B. Discussed his relationship with his wife with prisoners.
   C. Mention of the bowling score was not important, but this was an opening for the prisoners to make an insulting remark.
8. C
9. C
10. B
11. B
12. C
13. B
14. E
15. D
16. A. Deliver food while it is hot
    B. Supervisor must accompany the prisoner who is serving food
    C. Count utensils to and from prisoners
    D. Make seconds available as a means of preventing stronger prisoners from stealing food from the weak.
17. A
18. A. Do not diagnose.
    B. Supervise prisoners closely when they are taking medication.
    C. Never give out more than one dose of medication at one time.
    D. Keep accurate medical records.
    E. Permit all prisoners' sick call requests.
19. C
20. B
21. D
22. A. Escape record and detainers
    B. Work habits
    C. Behavior in confinement
23. A. To prevent adults from possibly sexually assaulting them.
    B. To keep juveniles from being exposed to hardened criminal types
24. There is no basic difference. The same principles and techniques can be used. Women must be kept separate from male prisoners.
25. C
26. A. Do not remove cuffs unless prior approval has been given by the jail administrator.
    B. Keep the prisoner in sight at all times.
    C. No special visits or other requests to be granted.

# TEST 5

DIRECTIONS: Each question or incomplete statement is followed by several suggested answers or completions. Select the one that BEST answers the question or completes the statement. *PRINT THE LETTER OF THE CORRECT ANSWER IN THE SPACE AT THE RIGHT.*

1. The GOAL of discipline in jail is to 1.____

   A. teach prisoners absolute obedience to orders
   B. teach acceptable behavior
   C. teach prisoners self-control
   D. control prisoners

2. Written rules serve the following purposes: 2.____
   I. To inform prisoners what not to do
   II. To inform prisoners about what is expected of them
   III. To establish standards for evaluating prisoners' conduct
   IV. Take authority away from jail officers who should be responsible for establishing standards of conduct

   The CORRECT answer is:

   A. I, II
   B. I, III
   C. II, IV
   D. III, IV
   E. II, III

3. Officer O has a temper that he displays whenever a prisoner gets on his nerves. He insists that prisoners do what they are told and that they follow the rules to the letter. It is his opinion that generally people get into trouble with the law because they lack discipline. He feels that it is his responsibility to teach prisoners discipline. 3.____
   Do you feel that Officer O is CORRECT?

   A. *Yes;* prisoners will generally take advantage of an officer who is not very strict.
   B. *No;* Officer O is too strict. He probably antagonizes prisoners by his attitude.
   C. *Yes;* all jail officers have a responsibility to teach prisoners discipline.
   D. *Yes;* however, he certainly sets a poor example by his display of temper.

4. Officer A caught two prisoners horsing around and decided to punish them by making them run in place. He reasoned that this would tire them so that they would not have the energy for horseplay. 4.____
   Do you think his actions were PROPER?

   A. *Yes;* prisoners learn a lesson from immediate punishment.
   B. *No;* the officer who sees the infraction should not, as a rule, also decide the punishment.
   C. Both of the above
   D. None of the above

5. Officer S is a firm believer in keeping order. He practices this belief and, as a result, turns in a high number of disciplinary reports. 5.____
   Do you think that S is acting properly?

   A. *Yes;* all infractions of rules should be reported.
   B. *No;* he should only report infractions that are serious and that cannot be handled informally.
   C. Both of the above
   D. None of the above

6. The following is a list of rule violations. Indicate those that require formal action and those that may be handled informally. (Use letter F for formal and letter I for informal.) 6.

A. Loud and continuous noise A.____
B. Talking after lights out B.____
C. Horseplay in sick call line C.____
D. Arguing with waiter in serving line D.____
E. Evidence of bar tampering E.____
F. Contraband (knife) F.____
G. Contraband (money) G.____
H. Contraband (book) H.____
I. Holding up line when returning to cells I.____

7. Officer D has taken Prisoner E out of line for horseplay and is correcting him before a group of interested prisoners. What do you think are the possible consequences of this action? 7.____

A. Prisoner E will learn a lesson.
B. Prisoner E may become angry at being embarrassed in front of other prisoners.
C. Officer D has realized that this was an excellent opportunity to teach E proper behavior and will make a positive impression on the prisoner.
D. The other prisoners will also have an opportunity to learn from Prisoner E's experience.

8. Prisoner O became abusive toward another prisoner, and they were on the edge of fighting when Officer C arrived on the scene. Both prisoners continued to argue, and a shoving contest began. 8.____
What should Officer C do?

A. Step between the prisoners and separate them.
B. Grab Prisoner O and pull him away.
C. Shout to both prisoners to stop.
D. He had better call another officer for assistance and then step in.

9. Officer S is a large man and quite sure of himself. Today, when Prisoner N refused to come out of his cell to take a shower, Officer S went in and took him out. 9.____
Do you think this was the proper method?

A. *Yes;* prisoners should do what they are told.
B. *No;* the prisoner should have been permitted to remain in his cell until he decided to come out.
C. *Yes;* prisoners must conform to all schedules.
D. If it was necessary that Prisoner N come out of his cell, the officer should not have gone in alone to take him out.

10. Prisoner N has declared that he is on a hunger strike and has refused to eat three meals in a row. A number of officers are upset by N's behavior and feel that something should be done about him. 10.____
Which do you feel is the PROPER procedure?

A. Force feed him; all prisoners should eat three meals a day.
B. Ignore him; he will eat when he is hungry.
C. Wait a few days; and if he continues to refuse food, he should be force fed.
D. Refer him to the doctor who can make a decision if and when he will require any medical care and forced feeding.

# KEY (CORRECT ANSWERS)

1. C
2. E
3. D
4. B
5. B
6. Formal: E, F, G, H
Informal: A, B, C, D
7. B
8. D
9. D
10. D

# TEST 6

DIRECTIONS: Each question or incomplete statement is followed by several suggested answers or completions. Select the one that BEST answers the question or completes the statement. *PRINT THE LETTER OF THE CORRECT ANSWER IN THE SPACE AT THE RIGHT.*

1. A prisoner is brought to the jail with the following symptoms: shakiness, staggering, thick speech, and a blank glassy-eyed look. 1.____
   Select the PROPER action to be taken.

   A. He is drunk; place him in the drunk tank.
   B. Although he may be drunk, it is possible that he may have a serious injury or illness. He should be referred to a doctor.
   C. Both of the above
   D. None of the above

2. Shortly after being admitted, a prisoner begins to shake, does not talk clearly, and claims to see bugs crawling over him. 2.____
   The jailer should do one of the following:

   A. The prisoner is obviously psychotic and should be referred to the doctor
   B. The prisoner is having *DTs;* the doctor should be called immediately
   C. Although the prisoner is acting strangely, he should be observed for a time until it is obvious that he is sick
   D. None of the above

3. Prisoner E has been in jail two weeks waiting trial. Lately, he has been acting strangely. He has been talking to an imaginary person, laughing and arguing. Today he accused Officer T of trying to *get him.* 3.____
   What should the officer do?

   A. Observe Prisoner E and submit a report to the administrator for medical referral
   B. Warn E to quiet down because he is disturbing others
   C. Try to prove to Prisoner E that the officer is not trying to get him
   D. None of the above

4. Prisoner L seems to have a habit of talking to himself, especially when he is playing solitaire. During the last week, he has also been complaining about his physical condition, claiming that he has a bad heart and that he is afraid it will stop one of these days soon. 4.____
   What should the officer do?

   A. It seems that L is becoming psychotic; he should be referred to the doctor.
   B. L's talking to himself is not a symptom of psychosis, but his physical complaint is; write a report and refer him to the doctor.
   C. There is nothing wrong with L; and since he has not requested medical attention, he should be left alone.
   D. Write a report on his complaints and refer him to the doctor. He may not be psychotic, but his medical complaint should be referred.

5. Prisoner V is charged with petty theft. Apparently, he absent-mindedly walked out of a store with a pair of gloves. Now he claims that he is innocent because he had money to pay for the gloves. Furthermore, he says that he has a bank account with ten thousand dollars. The other prisoners laugh at him, which only makes him angry. Since he has no money and no family, he has not called anyone. Now he wants an attorney and wants to call the largest bank in town for a release of funds. 5.____
What should the officer do?

   A. It is obvious that V is senile. He demonstrated this by forgetting he had the gloves when he left the store. Refer to the doctor.
   B. V is hallucinating; he certainly does not behave as though he has money. Refuse him permission to call the bank and refer to the doctor.
   C. Have V give his account number or other method of identifying himself and call the bank. If he has no account, refer to the doctor.
   D. None of the above

6. Officer Y has been watching Prisoner O for the last few days because he felt that O was acting strange. He finally sent a referral memo to the jail administrator that contained the following information: *Prisoner O has been acting strangely the last few days. He seems frightened, mumbles to himself, and walks the floor of his cell a lot. I think he should be seen by the doctor.* 6.____
Do you think this report contains sufficient information?

   A. *Yes;* it tells the doctor that the prisoner is acting strangely.
   B. *No;* there is not enough information.
   C. *Yes;* even though there is little information, there is enough for a doctor to know that something is wrong with the prisoner.
   D. *No;* there is very little description. It does not describe how the prisoner acts when frightened, how much walking is a lot, or contain any information that might show if the prisoner is talking to himself or hallucinating.

7. Prisoner G is very forgetful; he can't remember simple rules or follow instructions too well. He is a disciplinary problem because he always seems to be involved in some kind of illegal activity. Yesterday, he was caught with a knife. He claimed he was only carrying it for Prisoner B and claimed he did not know it is contraband. G is a youthful appearing 25 years. 7.____
What action should be taken?

   A. G is suffering from extreme advanced senility; refer him for a medical exam.
   B. G is a good liar and is only trying to get out of trouble now that he has been caught.
   C. G seems to be mentally deficient. Rather than harsh punishment, he needs to have someone explain rules to him more clearly. He also needs closer supervision.
   D. None of the above

8. Prisoner J appeared normal when he was admitted to the jail two days ago. Now he seems to be ill. He complains of aching muscles, is weak, and has lost his appetite, and is vomiting. 8.____
What seems to be his problem and what should the officer do?

   A. Sounds like flu; refer to the doctor.
   B. J is having drug withdrawal symptoms. He should be referred to the doctor, kept isolated from others, and closely supervised.
   C. J is suffering from insulin shock. He should be kept in a cell away from others until he calms down in a few days.
   D. Sounds like nothing. None of the above.

9. A person on drug withdrawal requires special care, including isolation and close supervision because 9.____

   A. drug addicts are usually dangerous and should always be housed in maximum security conditions
   B. he needs to be closely supervised to keep him away from drugs
   C. to prevent him from bothering others, to make it easier to control him, provide close supervision in case he attempts to injure himself
   D. all of the above

10. Officer D has on a number of occasions referred to *sex fiends* and how it is necessary to exercise care when around them because they are dangerous.
Do you agree? 10.____

   A. *Yes;* it is not possible to predict just what a sex offender will do.
   B. *No*; sex offenders are not dangerous while in jail, but I wouldn't want to meet one on the street.
   C. *Yes;* anyone who would commit sex crimes must be untrustworthy and dangerous.
   D. *No*; there are all types of sex offenders, and only a few are violent or dangerous.

11. Officer H has worked in the jail for many years. He is rightfully proud of his ability and experience. He claims that he can always spot a homosexual by his walk and feminine behavior.
Do you think that Officer H is CORRECT? 11.____

   A. *Yes;* all hmosexuals walk like girls and act feminine.
   B. *No;* it is not possible to identify a homosexual without interviewing him.
   C. *Yes;* it's very simple. They are usually slim and have delicate features.
   D. *No;* some masculine-appearing men are homosexual, and often slim delicately-built men are not. It is not appearance but behavior that must be examined.

12. Prisoner Y is slim and has a limp-wristed feminine appearance. Prisoner W is husky and aggressive. Y pretty much minds his own business and does his time. W is loud and is trying very hard to become friends with Y. He keeps offering Y cigarettes and candy which Y refuses. What do you suspect is happening? 12.____

   A. Nothing; W is just trying to be friendly.
   B. Obviously Y is homosexual and W doesn't seem to realize it.
   C. Y may or may not be a homosexual; his behavior so far does not indicate that he is. W, however, is acting like an aggressive homosexual and trying to get close to Y.
   D. None of the above

13. Indicate whether the following statements are TRUE or FALSE: 13.

   A. Homosexuals can be easily identified. A.____
   B. A person who talks to himself is psychotic. B.____
   C. People who threaten suicide will not attempt it. C.____
   D. People who threaten suicide are just trying to get sympathy. D.____
   E. Young people have a high suicide rate. E.____
   F. The best method of handling a person who threatens suicide is to call his bluff. F.____
   G. Keeping suicide risks isolated from others is the best way to manage them G.____

14. Prisoner K appears sick. His face is flushed, his skin is dry, and his mouth is dry. His breath is noticeably sweet. 14.____
What should you do?

A. Give him some aspirin and permit him to go on sick call.
B. Give him orange juice or something else with sugar in it because he is having insulin shock.
C. Call the doctor immediately; he is suffering from inadequate insulin.
D. Ignore the matter.

15. Prisoner P complains of not feeling well. He is pale and weak, his skin is moist, and he seems to be quite shaky as though he were intoxicated. P claims he is diabetic and is in need of something with sugar in it to correct this condition. 15.____
What would you do?

A. Check the records and, if they show he is diabetic, call the doctor and ask for instructions.
B. Ignore him because this is just another way for some prisoners to get something extra to eat.
C. Give him candy or orange juice; he is showing symptoms of insulin shock. If he does not feel better almost at once, call the doctor.
D. Give him the back of your hand.

16. Prisoner J is having a seizure in his cell. 16.____
What should the officer do? (Select five.)

A. Hold him down so that he does not injure himself.
B. Remove nearby objects so that he does not injure himself.
C. Sit him up and give him water to drink.
D. Wait until the seizure is over and then give him his medication.
E. Loosen clothing around neck and place a padded object between his teeth to prevent his biting his tongue.
F. Place coat or pillow beneath prisoner's head to prevent injury.
G. Turn his face to one side.
H. Notify the doctor immediately.
I. The doctor should be routinely informed.

17. Prisoner J has had four seizures in the last hour. You have followed the proper procedure in helping him in each instance. 17.____
What do you do NEXT?

A. Make certain that he is taking his medication.
B. Restrain him on his bed so that he does not injure himself during the next seizure.
C. Call the doctor immediately in order to provide emergency care.
D. All of the above

18. As a result of a seizure, Prisoner J has received a head injury. The wound located above the right ear is bleeding. In addition, there seems to be watery fluid flowing from his nose. His breathing is slow and difficult. As yet, he has not regained consciousness as he usually does immediately after a seizure. 18.____
What should you do?

A. Let him sleep; he must be tired from the seizure.
B. Apply a pressure bandage to stop the bleeding.
C. Call the doctor; there seems to be evidence that he may have a serious head wound.
D. Call the warden.
E. Nothing; he's trying to divert your attention.

19. The jail officer's responsibility in managing special prisoners includes the following areas: (Select four.) 19.____

A. Diagnosing prisoners' physical and mental condition and referring to the doctor.
B. Giving first aid whenever it is needed.
C. Noticing strange or unusual behavior and referring to the doctor.
D. Developing the ability to describe the physical and emotional condition of prisoners objectively.
E. Prepare records that describe prisoners' injuries and record their medical complaints.
F. Evaluate prisoner medical complaints, prescribe medication when required, and keep the chronic complainers from sick call.
G. Closely supervise the taking of medication, keep careful records of all medicine distributed to and taken by prisoners.

---

# KEY (CORRECT ANSWERS)

1. B
2. B
3. A
4. D
5. C

6. D
7. C
8. B
9. C
10. D

11. D
12. C
13. A. F
    B. F
    C. F
    D. F
    E. T
    F. F
    G. F
14. C
15. C

16. B, E, F, G, I
17. C
18. C
19. C, D, E, G

---

# READING COMPREHENSION
# UNDERSTANDING AND INTERPRETING WRITTEN MATERIAL

## EXAMINATION SECTION

## TEST 1

DIRECTIONS: Each question or incomplete statement is followed by several suggested answers or completions. Select the one that BEST answers the question or completes the statement. *PRINT THE LETTER OF THE CORRECT ANSWER IN THE SPACE AT THE RIGHT.*

Questions 1-3.

DIRECTIONS: Questions 1 through 3 are to be answered SOLELY on the basis of the following passage.

The basic disparity between punitive and correctional crime control should be noted. The first explicitly or implicitly assumes the availability of choice or freedom of the will and asserts the responsibility of the individual for what he does. Thus, the concept of punishment has both a moral and practical justification. However, correctional crime control, though also deterministic in outlook, either explicitly or implicitly considers criminal behavior as the result of conditions and factors present in the individual or his environment; it does not think in terms of free choices available to the individual and his resultant responsibility, but rather in terms of the removal of the criminogenic conditions for which the individual may not be responsible and over which he may not have any control. Some efforts have been made to achieve a theoretical reconciliation of these two rather diametrically opposed approaches but this has not been accomplished, and their coexistence in practice remains an unresolved contradiction.

1. According to the *correctional* view of crime control mentioned in the above passage, criminal behavior is the result of 1.____
   A. environmental factors for which individuals should be held responsible
   B. harmful environmental factors which should be eliminated
   C. an individual's choice for which he should be held responsible and punished
   D. an individual's choice and can be corrected in a therapeutic environment

2. According to the above passage, the one of the following which is a problem in correctional practice is 2.____
   A. identifying emotionally disturbed individuals
   B. determining effective punishment for criminal behavior
   C. reconciling the punitive and correctional views of crime control
   D. assuming that a criminal is the product of his environment and has no free will

3. According to the above passage, the one of the following which is an ASSUMPTION underlying the punitive crime control viewpoint rather than the correctional viewpoint is that crime is caused by 3.____

A. inherited personality traits
B. poor socio-economic background
C. lack of parental guidance
D. irresponsibility on the part of the individual

Questions 4-9.

DIRECTIONS: Questions 4 through 9 are to be answered SOLELY on the basis of the following passage.

Man's historical approach to criminals can be conveniently summarized as a succession of three R's: Revenge, Restraint, and Reformation. Revenge was the primary response prior to the first revolution in penology in the 18th and 19th centuries. It was replaced during that revolution by an emphasis upon restraint. When the second revolution occurred in the late 19th and 20th centuries, reformation became an important objective. Attention was focused upon the mental and emotional makeup of the offender and efforts were made to alter these as the primary sources of difficulty.

We have now entered yet another revolution in which a fourth concept has been added to the list of R's: Reintegration. This has come about because students of corrections feel that a singular focus upon reforming the offender is inadequate. Successful rehabilitation is a two-sided coin, including reformation on one side and reintegration on the other.

It can be argued that the third revolution is premature. Society itself is still very ambivalent about the offender. It has never really replaced all vestiges of revenge or restraint, simply supplemented them. Thus, while it is unwilling to kill or lock up all offenders permanently, it is also unwilling to give full support to the search for alternatives.

4. According to the above passage, revolutions against accepted treatment of criminals have resulted in all of the following approaches to handling criminals EXCEPT 4.____
A. revenge B. restraint C. reformation D. reintegration

5. According to the above passage, society NOW views the offender with 5.____
A. uncertainty B. hatred C. sympathy D. acceptance

6. According to the above passage, the second revolution directed PARTICULAR attention to 6.____
A. preparing the offender for his return to society
B. making the pain of punishment exceed the pleasure of crime
C. exploring the inner feelings of the offender
D. restraining the offender from continuing his life of crime

7. According to the above passage, students of corrections feel that the lack of success of rehabilitation programs is due to 7.____
A. the mental and emotional makeup of the offender
B. vestiges of revenge and restraint which linger in correction programs
C. failure to achieve reintegration together with reformation
D. premature planning of the third revolution

8. The above passage suggests that the latest revolution will 8.____
   A. fail and the cycle will begin again with revenge or restraint
   B. be the last revolution
   C. not work unless correctional goals can be defined
   D. succumb to political and economic pressures

9. The one of the following titles which BEST expresses the main idea of the above passage is 9.____
   A. IS CRIMINAL JUSTICE ENOUGH?
   B. APPROACHES IN THE TREATMENT OF THE CRIMINAL OFFENDER
   C. THE THREE R'S IN CRIMINAL REFORMATION
   D. MENTAL DISEASE FACTORS IN THE CRIMINAL CORRECTION SYSTEM

Questions 10-15.

DIRECTIONS: Questions 10 through 15 are to be answered SOLELY on the basis of the following passage.

In a study by J.E. Cowden, an attempt was made to determine which variables would best predict institutional adjustment and recidivism in recently committed delinquent boys. The results suggested in particular that older boys, when first institutionalized, who are initially rated as being more mature and more amenable to change, will most likely adjust better than the average boy adjusts to the institution. Prediction of institutional adjustment was rendered slightly more accurate by using the variables of age and personality prognosis in combined form.

With reference to the prediction of recidivism, boys who committed more serious offenses showed less recidivism than average. These boys were also older than average when first committed. The variable of age accounts in part for both their more serious offenses and for their lower subsequent rate of recidivism.

The results also showed some trends suggesting that boys from higher socio-economic b backgrounds tended to commit more serious offenses leading to their institutionalization as delinquents. However, neither the ratings of socio-economic status nor *home-environment* appeared to be significantly related to recidivism in this study.

Cowden also found an essentially linear relationship between personality prognosis and recidivism, and between institutional adjustment and recidivism. When these variables were used jointly to predict recidivism, accuracy of prediction was increased only slightly, but in general the ability to predict recidivism fell far below the ability to predict institutional adjustment.

10. According to the above passage, which one of the following was NOT found to be a significant factor in predicting recidivism? 10.____
   A. Age
   B. Personality
   C. Socio-economic background
   D. Institutional adjustment

11. According to the above passage, institutional adjustment was MORE accurately predicted when the variables used were 11.____
   A. socio-economic background and recidivism
   B. recidivism and personality
   C. personality and age
   D. age and socio-economic background

12. According to the above passage, which of the following were variables in predicting both recidivism and institutional adjustment? 12.____
    A. Age and personality
    B. Family background and age
    C. Nature of offense and age
    D. Personality

13. Which one of the following conclusions is MOST justified by the above passage? 13.____
    A. Institutional adjustment had a lower level of predictability and recidivism.
    B. Recidivism and seriousness of offense are negatively correlated to some degree.
    C. Institutional adjustment and personality prognosis, when considered together, are significantly better predictors of recidivism than either one alone.
    D. A delinquent boy from a lower class family background is more likely to have committed a serious first offense than a delinquent boy from a higher socio-economic background.

14. The study discussed in the above passage found that delinquent boys from a higher socio-economic background tended to 14.____
    A. commit more serious crimes
    B. commit less serious crimes
    C. show more recidivism than average
    D. show less recidivism than average

15. The MOST appropriate conclusion to be drawn from the study discussed above is that 15.____
    A. delinquent boys from higher socio-economic backgrounds show less institutional adjustment than average
    B. a high positive correlation was found between recidivism and institutional adjustment
    C. home environment, although not significantly related to recidivism, did influence institutional adjustment
    D. older boys are more likely to commit more serious first offenses and show less recidivism than younger boys

Questions 16-18.

DIRECTIONS: Questions 16 through 18 are to be answered SOLELY on the basis of the following passage.

Educational programming of the offender has become part of the dominant philosophy in the correctional community. Due to the recent increase in national funding for demonstration prison education projects, future research endeavors may well be facilitated so that we can better evaluate the effectiveness of specific educational approaches. Research on past programs has resulted in various conclusions as to their effectiveness in the reduction of recidivism. Even though some programs have seemed promising, when they are properly evaluated, the initial results have been found to be spurious. Invalidity stemmed, by and large, from the fact that inmates shown to be *successful* in such educational programs may have *had it made* anyway, particularly when those selected for the program were the best risks. Success of the program was judged on the basis of a study of recidivism which, due to lack of funds, was of insufficient duration.

Research is the bookkeeping of corrections. Unfortunately, many correctional enterprises operate without such bookkeeping. When this happens, like businesses without bookkeeping, they may soon be bankrupt. However, unlike business, corrections can provide a steady salary for its employees even when it is bankrupt.

Despite these sad conclusions, effective program implementation can become a reality through continued experimentation and evaluation, utilizing acceptable methodological procedures and specially trained personnel, as well as having the necessary total institutional support.

16. According to the above passage, the apparent success of past correctional educational programs was due in LARGE part to 16.____
    A. biased samples
    B. competent trainers
    C. societal acceptance
    D. inferior goals

17. The second paragraph in the above passage states that *Research is the bookkeeping of corrections.* 17.____
    Which of the following MOST accurately describes what is meant by this statement?
    A. Since correctional facilities are government institutions, only records of government research grants and the use of those grants can indicate when the institution is in financial difficulty.
    B. Research provides to correctional institutions information which is essential for their decision-making.
    C. Without grants for research, correctional institutions will become financially bankrupt even though they are still able to pay employee salaries.
    D. Correctional institutions must keep abreast of research or they will find themselves educationally bankrupt.

18. According to the above passage, the future of educational programming is brighter than its past because of 18.____
    A. social awareness
    B. longer programs
    C. increased national funding
    D. more highly qualified administrators

Questions 19-23.

DIRECTIONS: Questions 19 through 23 are to be answered SOLELY on the basis of the following passage.

The social problems created by the urban delinquent gang member require the attention and resources of the entire community. Recent studies have shown that we are dealing with a boy who early in life has his first official contact with the police and who, shortly afterwards, is bound for juvenile court. The gang member commits several delinquencies before reaching adult status and the earlier his onset of delinquency, the more serious become his violations of the law. There is also evidence of increasingly serious delinquency involvement of a substantial proportion of the gang members. Of major significance are the shorter periods of time between each succeeding offense and the delinquents; employment or threat to employ force and violence.

All of these findings testify to the urgent need for prevention and treatment to be directed at pre- and early adolescence and to be sensitive to the importance of the first signs of youthful disregard for society's legal norms. Follow-up studies on delinquent gang members revealed that forty percent of the gang members continued into adult crime. For several reasons, this is a minimal figure and should probably be twenty percent higher. It is reasonable to infer that, given more thorough follow-up techniques and a longer follow-up period, an appreciable number of those for whom no criminal records were located will acquire them. In any event, these studies have revealed a strong linkage between delinquency and crime. This linkage has been established by following up a group of gang members into adulthood rather than by tracing back a group of adult offenders into delinquency, and by utilizing a sample of juveniles dealt with by the police rather than those appearing before a juvenile court, or in a clinic.

19. According to the above passage, as delinquents get older, their crimes GENERALLY become _____ serious _____ frequent. 19.____
   A. more; and more
   B. more; but less
   C. less; but more
   D. less; and less

20. The above passage SUGGESTS that delinquents should receive 20.____
   A. severe punishment at the time of their first offense
   B. institutional care until such time that they may prove themselves capable of functioning in a free society
   C. treatment at pre- and early adolescence at the first signs of disregard for societal norms
   D. continuous psychological counseling from the time of their first offense until the delinquent reaches legal age

21. According to the above passage, delinquent gang members pose a problem which should be the responsibility of the 21.____
   A. community
   B. police
   C. courts
   D. social worker

22. According to the above passage, follow-up studies on delinquent gang members have underestimated the percent of gang members who continued to adult crime because 22.____
   A. their sample was biased as it only involved urban gang members
   B. the studies did not follow the *career* of the sample group for a long enough period of time
   C. the studies concerned only those juveniles who, as adults, were dealt with by the police and not those who appeared in court or were referred to a clinic
   D. the method used, that of following up a group of gang members rather than tracing back a group of adult offenders, was invalid

23. According to the above passage, the actual percent of delinquent gang members who continue into adult crime is MOST NEARLY 23.____
   A. 20%
   B. 40%
   C. 50%
   D. 60%

Questions 24-25.

DIRECTIONS: Questions 24 through 25 are to be answered SOLELY on the basis of the following passage.

The criminal justice system is generally regarded as having the basic objective of reducing crime. However, one must also consider its larger objective of minimizing the total social costs associated with crime and crime control. Both of these components are complex and difficult to measure completely. The social costs associated with crime come from the long- and short-term physical damage, psychological harm, and property losses to victims as a result of crimes committed. Crime also creates serious indirect effects. It can induce a feeling of insecurity that is only partially reflected in business losses and economic disruption due to anxiety about venturing into high crime rate areas.

Balanced against these costs associated with crime must be the consequences of actions taken to reduce them. Money spent on developing, maintaining, and operating criminal justice agencies is part of the cost of the crime control system. But there are also indirect costs, such as welfare payments to prisoners' families, income lost by offenders who are denied good jobs, legal fees, and wages lost by witnesses. In addition, there are penalties suffered by suspects erroneously arrested or sentenced, the limitation on personal liability resulting from police surveillance, and the invasion of privacy in maintaining criminal records.

24. According to the above passage, all of the following are indirect costs of the crime control system EXCEPT 24.____
    A. wages lost by witnesses
    B. money spent for legal services
    C. payments made to the families of prisoners
    D. money spent on operating criminal justice agencies

25. According to the above passage, actions taken to reduce crime 25.____
    A. will reduce the indirect costs of the crime control system
    B. may result in a decrease of personal liberty
    C. may cause psychological harm to victims of crime
    D. should immediately start improving the criminal justice system

# KEY (CORRECT ANSWERS)

| | | | |
|---|---|---|---|
| 1. | B | 11. | C |
| 2. | C | 12. | A |
| 3. | D | 13. | B |
| 4. | A | 14. | A |
| 5. | A | 15. | D |
| 6. | C | 16. | A |
| 7. | C | 17. | B |
| 8. | C | 18. | C |
| 9. | B | 19. | A |
| 10. | C | 20. | C |

| | |
|---|---|
| 21. | A |
| 22. | B |
| 23. | D |
| 24. | D |
| 25. | B |

# TEST 2

DIRECTIONS: Each question or incomplete statement is followed by several suggested answers or completions. Select the one that BEST answers the question or completes the statement. *PRINT THE LETTER OF THE CORRECT ANSWER IN THE SPACE AT THE RIGHT.*

Questions 1-4.

DIRECTIONS: Questions 1 through 4 are to be answered SOLELY on the basis of the following passage.

The initial contact between the offender and the correctional social worker frequently occurs at the point of extreme crisis, when the usual adaptive mechanisms have been broken down. In many areas of correctional practice, such as probation and parole, this contact is often followed by long periods during which limited freedom is officially imposed. It is at such points that response to the offer of hope for restoring equilibrium may mean most, and that new coping capacities and new person-environment relationships develop. As a result, many correctional social workers have become skilled in strategies of crisis intervention. What they learn from such endeavors does not generally find its way into the professional literature; thus, the correctional social worker has contributed little to developing and testing practice theory. However, beginning efforts are being made to remedy this situation, and it is probable that corrections may provide an important laboratory from which tomorrow's understanding of the theory and strategies of crisis intervention will emerge.

1. Which of the following is the MOST appropriate title for the above passage? 1.____
   A. CORRECTIONAL SOCIAL WORK IN CRISIS
   B. CRISIS INTERVENTION AND CORRECTIONAL SOCIAL WORK
   C. COPING CAPACITIES OF PROBATIONERS AND PAROLEES
   D. THE THEORY AND PRACTICE OF CRISIS INTERVENTION

2. It can be concluded from the above passage that crisis intervention as a method of treatment and rehabilitation in correctional social work is based on the premise that a(n) 2.____
   A. offender may be more likely to respond to help and change his lifestyle a a time of crisis, such as being on probation or parole, when incarceration is the only other alternative
   B. person is not likely to respond to help and change his lifestyle unless he is in a crisis situation, such as being on probation or parole, when he is threatened by imprisonment
   C. offender sentenced to probation or parole is likely to respond to help and change his lifestyle, because his freedom is limited and supervision is imposed on him
   D. situation such as probation or parole, in which an offender is supervised and his freedom is limited, presents ideal conditions for constructive personality change

3. On the basis of the above passage, it would be VALID to assume that 3.____
   A. offenders sentenced to probation and parole usually develop coping capacities which would not emerge during imprisonment
   B. offenders who are rehabilitated as a result of probation and parole have greater coping capacities in crisis situations
   C. a life crisis situation such as being sentenced to probation or parole may become a positive force toward an offender's rehabilitation
   D. an offender's ability to develop new coping capacities in times of crisis should be a decisive factor in determining the recommended sentence

4. According to the above passage, correctional social workers' experiences in crisis intervention have 4.____
   A. encouraged use of crisis intervention strategy
   B. contributed to theory rather than practice
   C. not resulted in further learning
   D. not generally been reported in print

Questions 5-9.

DIRECTIONS: Questions 5 through 9 are to be answered SOLELY on the basis of the following passage.

The group worker must be concerned with two major goals in correctional treatment of juvenile offenders: (a) sustaining and reinforcing conventional value systems, and (b) enhancing the youth's positive self-image and general feeling of worthiness. The group processes involved in working toward these ends are so interrelated that treatment can meet both goals by improving interpersonal skills and experiences. As an initial concept, it is important to recognize that, in spite of delinquent behavior, adolescents usually do exhibit conscience formation, as may be seen in their support of conformity values, evidence of guilt and conventional behavior, and rationalization of delinquent behavior. It is this very ambivalence toward the conventional order that can be the basis for rehabilitation. On the basis of the distinction between real guilt and guilt reflecting emotional problems, an ideal therapeutic objective is to reach the point at which the internal and external controls are in general harmony and agency expectations are closely allied to and consistent with group and individual expectations.

5. Which of the following is the BEST title for the above passage? 5.____
   A. GROUP TREATMENT OF JUVENILE OFFENDERS
   B. THE GROUP WORKER AND CORRECTIONAL TREATMENT
   C. THE JUVENILE OFFENDER
   D. CONSCIENCE FORMATION IN JUVENILE OFFENDERS

6. On the basis of the above passage, it would be VALID to assume that group treatment of the juvenile offender can result in the development of 6.____
   A. greater self-confidence
   B. rationalization of delinquent behavior
   C. guilt and conscience formation
   D. increased conscientiousness

7. On the basis of the above statement, it would be VALID to conclude that juvenile offenders 7.____
   A. are anxious for rehabilitation
   B. have no internal or external controls
   C. are deficient in interpersonal skills and experiences
   D. feel more guilt because of emotional problems than because of offenses committed

8. According to the above passage, a characteristic of juvenile offenders which makes them amenable to correctional treatment is that they 8.____
   A. can be reached by group processes
   B. have a general feeling of worthiness
   C. show signs of conscience formation
   D. are ambivalent toward rehabilitation

9. According to the above passage, an IDEAL therapeutic objective in the group treatment of juvenile offenders would be based on 9.____
   A. agency expectations
   B. group expectations
   C. the distinction between real guilt and irrational guilt
   D. the harmony between external and internal controls

Questions 10-14.

DIRECTIONS: Questions 10 through 14 are to be answered SOLELY on the basis of the following passage.

Mental disorders are found in a fairly large number of the inmates in correctional institutions. There are no exact figures as to the number of inmates who are mentally disturbed—partly because it is hard to draw a precise line between *mental disturbance* and *normality*—but experts find that somewhere between 15% and 25% of inmates are suffering from disorders that are obvious enough to show up in routine psychiatric examinations. Society has not yet really come to grips with the problem of what to do with mentally disturbed offenders. There is not enough money available to set up treatment programs for all the people identified as mentally disturbed; and there would probably not be enough qualified psychiatric personnel available to run such programs even if they could be set up. Most mentally disturbed offenders are, therefore, left to serve out their time in correctional institutions, and the burden of dealing with them falls on correction officers. This means that a correction officer must be sensitive enough to human behavior to know when he is dealing with a person who is not mentally normal, and that the officer must be imaginative enough to be able to sense how an abnormal individual might react under certain circumstances.

10. According to the above passage, mentally disturbed inmates in correctional institutions 10.____
    A. are usually transferred to mental hospitals when their condition is noticed
    B. cannot be told from other inmates because tests cannot distinguish between sane people and normal people
    C. may constitute as much as 25% of the total inmate population
    D. should be regarded as no different from all the other inmates

11. The above passage says that today the job of handling mentally disturbed inmates is MAINLY up to 11.____
   A. psychiatric personnel
   B. other inmates
   C. correction officers
   D. administrative officials

12. Of the following, which is a reason given in the passage for society's failure to provide adequate treatment programs for mentally disturbed inmates? 12.____
   A. Law-abiding citizens should not have to pay for fancy treatment programs for criminals.
   B. A person who breaks the law should not expect society to give him special help.
   C. It is impossible to tell whether an inmate is mentally disturbed.
   D. There are not enough trained people to provide the kind of treatment needed.

13. The expression *abnormal individual*, as used in the last sentence of the passage, refers to an individual who is 13.____
   A. of average intelligence
   B. of superior intelligence
   C. completely normal
   D. mentally disturbed

14. The reader of the passage would MOST likely agree that 14.____
   A. correction officers should not expect mentally disturbed persons to behave the same way a normal person would behave
   B. correction officers should not report infractions of the rules committed by mentally disturbed persons
   C. mentally disturbed persons who break the law should be treated exactly the same way as anyone else
   D. mentally disturbed persons who have broken the law should not be imprisoned

Questions 15-19.

DIRECTIONS: Questions 15 through 19 are to be answered SOLELY on the basis of the following passage.

When a young boy or girl is released from one of the various facilities operated by the Division for Youth, supportive services to help the youth face community, group, and family pressures are needed as much as, if not more than, at any other time. These services are the responsibility of two units of the Division for Youth, the Aftercare Unit, which serves youths discharged from the urban homes, camps, and START Centers, and the Community Service Bureaus, which serve youths released from the division's school and center programs. To assure that supportive services for released youths are easily identifiable and accessible, the division has developed the *store-front* services center, located in the heart of those areas to which many of the youngsters are returning. The storefront concept and structure is able to coordinate more closely services to the particular needs and situation of the youths and to draw on the feeling of community participation and achievement by persuading the community to join in helping them.

15. Of the following, the BEST description of the storefront services center's relationship to neighborhood residents is that it 15.____
   A. actively encourages their participation
   B. accepts their help when offered
   C. asks neighborhood residents to develop rehabilitation programs
   D. limits participation to qualified neighborhood professional youth workers

16. On the basis of the paragraph, which of the following statements is CORRECT? 16.____
   A. Supportive services are not needed as much after a youth is released from a facility as during his stay.
   B. Storefront services centers are located near the facilities operated by the Division for Youth
   C. The Community Service Bureaus serve youths released from urban homes.
   D. Youths are given supportive services in their communities after release from facilities operated by the Division for Youth

17. Of the following, the MOST suitable title for the above paragraph would be 17.____
   A. PROBLEMS OF YOUTHS RETURNING TO SOCIETY
   B. COMMUNITY, GROUP, AND FAMILY PRESSURES ON RELEASED YOUTHS
   C. NEIGHBORHOOD SUPPORTIVE SERVICES FOR RELEASED YOUTHS
   D. A SURVEY OF FACILITIES OPERATED BY THE DIVISION FOR YOUTH

18. Which of the following characteristics of the storefront services is mentioned in the above paragraph? 18.____
   A. Cost B. Availability C. Size D. Complexity

19. On the basis of the paragraph, which of the following statements about the Aftercare Unit is INCORRECT? 19.____
   It
   A. is a part of the Division for Youth
   B. serves youths released from school programs
   C. is similar in function to the Community Service Bureaus
   D. was partly responsible for the development of storefront centers

20. The intended purposes of imprisonment are to punish, to correct through fear of repeated punishment, to provide opportunity for penitence, and to protect society by isolating the criminal. In point of fact, other emotions—notably hate for and a desire for revenge against those responsible for their imprisonment—are a greater product of imprisonment than is fear. 20.____
   On the basis of this paragraph alone, the MOST accurate of the following conclusions is that
   A. a basis for further criminality is established by emotional factors resulting from previous imprisonment
   B. imprisonment will achieve its intended purpose only to the extent that it substitutes emotional reactions for logical thought

C. opportunities for penitence are made more necessary by the growth of a desire for revenge
D. society's protection is necessarily limited to the time an individual is imprisoned

21. The misconduct of juveniles is a symptom of some inner or outer disturbance, usually both. To the casual observer, his behavior may seem naughty or vicious, or both. To the delinquent himself, it has as much meaning as socially approved activity has for the well-behaved. 21.____
Misconduct, according to this statement,
A. has meaning to the delinquent only if it carries with it strong social disapproval
B. is resorted to in many cases as an attention-getter device to impress the casual observer
C. may result from personal maladjustments and is meaningful to the delinquent
D. stems from a juvenile's rejection of social approval for his normal activities

Questions 22-25.

DIRECTIONS: Questions 22 through 25 are to be answered SOLELY on the basis of the following passage.

There is controversy and misunderstanding about the proper function of juvenile courts and their probation departments. There are cries that the whole process produces delinquents rather than rehabilitates them. There are speeches by the score about *getting tough* with the kids. Another large group thinks we should be more understanding and gentle with delinquents. This distrust of the services offered can be attributed in large part to the confusion in the use of these services throughout the country.

On the one hand, the juvenile courts are tied to the criminal court system, with an obligation to decide guilt and innocence for offenses specifically stated and formally charged. On the other hand, they have the obligation to provide treatment, supervision, and guidance to youngsters in trouble, without respect to the crimes of which they are accused. These two conflicting assignments must be carried out—quite properly—in an informal, private way, which will not stigmatize a youngster during his formative years.

And, as the courts' preoccupation with the latter task has increased, the former (that of dispensing justice) has retreated, with the result that grave injustices are bound to occur.

22. The title below that BEST expresses the ideas of this passage is 22.____
A. A PROBLEM FOR TODAY'S TEENAGERS
B. REHABILITATING YOUTHFUL CRIMINALS
C. FITTING THE PUNISHMENT TO THE CRIME
D. JUSTICE FOR JUVENILE OFFENDERS

23. The author contends that public distrust of juvenile courts is PRIMARILY the result of 23.____
    A. the dual function of these courts
    B. lack of a sufficient number of probation officers
    C. injustices done by the courts
    D. the cost of keeping up the courts

24. The above passage suggests that the author 24.____
    A. is familiar with the problem
    B. is impatient with justice
    C. sides with those who favor leniency for juvenile offenders
    D. regards all offenses as equally important

25. The tone of the above passage is 25.____
    A. highly emotional
    B. highly personal
    C. optimistic
    D. calm

# KEY (CORRECT ANSWERS)

| | | | |
|---|---|---|---|
| 1. | B | 11. | C |
| 2. | A | 12. | D |
| 3. | C | 13. | D |
| 4. | D | 14. | A |
| 5. | A | 15. | A |
| 6. | A | 16. | D |
| 7. | C | 17. | C |
| 8. | C | 18. | B |
| 9. | C | 19. | B |
| 10. | C | 20. | A |

| | |
|---|---|
| 21. | C |
| 22. | D |
| 23. | A |
| 24. | A |
| 25. | D |

# PREPARING WRITTEN MATERIAL

## PARAGRAPH REARRANGEMENT COMMENTARY

The sentences that follow are in scrambled order. You are to rearrange them in proper order and indicate the letter choice containing the correct answer at the space at the right.

Each group of sentences in this section is actually a paragraph presented in scrambled order. Each sentence in the group has a place in that paragraph; no sentence is to be left out. You are to read each group of sentences and decide upon the best order in which to put the sentences so as to form a well-organized paragraph.

The questions in this section measure the ability to solve a problem when all the facts relevant to its solution are not given.

More specifically, certain positions of responsibility and authority require the employee to discover connection between events sometimes, apparently, unrelated. In order to do this, the employee will find it necessary to correctly infer that unspecified events have probably occurred or are likely to occur. This ability becomes especially important when action must be taken on incomplete information.

Accordingly, these questions require competitors to choose among several suggested alternatives, each of which presents a different sequential arrangement of the events. Competitors must choose the MOST logical of the suggested sequences.

In order to do so, they may be required to draw on general knowledge to infer missing concepts or events that are essential to sequencing the given events. Competitors should be careful to infer only what is essential to the sequence. The plausibility of the wrong alternatives will always require the inclusion of unlikely events or of additional chains of events which are NOT essential to sequencing the given events.

It's very important to remember that you are looking for the best of the four possible choices, and that the best choice of all may not even be one of the answers you're given to choose from.

There is no one right way to solve these problems. Many people have found it helpful to first write out the order of the sentences, as they would have arranged them, on their scrap paper before looking at the possible answers. If their optimum answer is there, this can save them some time. If it isn't, this method can still give insight into solving the problem. Others find it most helpful to just go through each of the possible choices, contrasting each as they go along. You should use whatever method feels comfortable and works for you.

While most of these types of questions are not that difficult, we've added a higher percentage of the difficult type, just to give you more practice. Usually there are only one or two questions on this section that contain such subtle distinctions that you're unable to answer confidently. And you then may find yourself stuck deciding between two possible choices, neither of which you're sure about.

---

# EXAMINATION SECTION

# TEST 1

DIRECTIONS: The sentences that follow are in scrambled order. You are to rearrange them in proper order and indicate the letter choice containing the correct answer. *PRINT THE LETTER OF THE CORRECT ANSWER IN THE SPACE AT THE RIGHT.*

1. Below are four statements labeled W, X, Y and Z. 1.____
   W. He was a strict and fanatic drillmaster.
   X. The word is always used in a derogatory sense and generally shows resentment and anger on the part of the user.
   Y. It is from the name of this Frenchman that we derive our English word, martinet.
   Z. Jean Martinet was the Inspector-General of Infantry during the reign of King Louis XIV.

   The PROPER order in which these sentences should be placed in a paragraph is:

   A. X, Z, W, Y B. X, Z, Y, W C. Z, W, Y, X D. Z, Y, W, X

2. In the following paragraph, the sentences, which are numbered, have been jumbled. 2.____
   I. Since then it has undergone changes.
   II. It was incorporated in 1955 under the laws of the State of New York.
   III. Its primary purposes, a cleaner city, has, however, remained the same.
   IV. The Citizens Committee works in cooperation with the Mayor's Inter-departmental Committee for a Clean City. 3.____

   The order in which these sentences should be arranged to form a well-organized paragraph is:

   A. II, IV, I, III B. III, IV, I, II C. IV, II, I, III D. IV, III, II, I

Questions 3-5.

DIRECTIONS: The sentences listed below are part of a meaningful paragraph but they are not given in their proper order. You are to decide what would be the BEST order in which to put the sentences so as to form a well-organized paragraph. Each sentence has a place in the paragraph; there are no extra sentences. You are then to answer Questions 3 through 5 inclusive on the basis of your rearrangements of these scrambled sentences into a properly organized paragraph.

In 1887 some insurance companies organized an Inspection Department to advise their clients on all phases of fire prevention and protection. Probably this has been due to the smaller annual fire losses in Great Britain than in the United States. It tests various fire prevention devices and appliances and determines manufacturing hazards and their safeguards. Fire research began earlier in the United States and is more advanced than in Great Britain. Later they established a laboratory specializing in electrical, mechanical, hydraulic, and chemical fields.

3. When the five sentences are arranged in proper order, the paragraph starts with the sentence which begins 3.____
   A. "In 1887..." B. "Probably this..." C. "It tests..."
   D. "Fire research..." E. "Later they..."

4. In the last sentence listed above, "they" refers to 4.____
   A. the insurance companies
   B. the United States and Great Britain
   C. the Inspection Department
   D. clients
   E. technicians

5. When the above paragraph is properly arranged, it ends with the words 5.____
   A. "...and protection."
   B. "...the United States."
   C. "...their safeguards."
   D. "...in Great Britain."
   E. "...chemical fields."

---

# KEY (CORRECT ANSWERS)

1. C
2. C
3. D
4. A
5. C

---

# TEST 2

DIRECTIONS: In each of the questions numbered I through V, several sentences are given. For each question, choose as your answer the group of number that represents the MOST logical order of these sentences if they were arranged in paragraph form. *PRINT THE LETTER OF THE CORRECT ANSWER IN THE SPACE AT THE RIGHT.*

1. I. It is established when one shows that the landlord has prevented the tenant's enjoyment of his interest in the property leased. 1.____
   II. Constructive eviction is the result of a breach of the covenant of quiet enjoyment implied in all leases.
   III. In some parts of the United States, it is not complete until the tenant vacates within a reasonable time.
   IV. Generally, the acts must be of such serious and permanent character as to deny the tenant the enjoyment of his possessing rights.
   V. In this event, upon abandonment of the premises, the tenant's liability for that ceases.

   The CORRECT answer is:
   A. II, I, IV, III, V  B. V, II, III, I, IV
   C. IV, III, I, II, V  D. I, III, V, IV, II

2. I. The powerlessness before private and public authorities that is the typical experience of the slum tenant is reminiscent of the situation of blue-collar workers all through the nineteenth century. 2.____
   II. Similarly, in recent years, this chapter of history has been reopened by anti-poverty groups which have attempted to organize slum tenants to enable them to bargain collectively with their landlords about the conditions of their tenancies.
   III. It is familiar history that many of the worker remedied their condition by joining together and presenting their demands collectively.
   IV. Like the workers, tenants are forced by the conditions of modern life into substantial dependence on these who possess great political aid and economic power.
   V. What's more, the very fact of dependence coupled with an absence of education and self-confidence makes them hesitant and unable to stand up for what they need from those in power.

   The CORRECT answer is:
   A. V, IV, I, II, III  B. II, III, I, V, IV
   C. III, I, V, IV, II  D. I, IV, V, III, II

3. I. A railroad, for example, when not acting as a common carrier may contract away responsibility for its own negligence. 3.____
   II. As to a landlord, however, no decision has been found relating to the legal effect of a clause shifting the statutory duty of repair to the tenant.
   III. The courts have not passed on the validity of clauses relieving the landlord of this duty and liability.
   IV. They have, however, upheld the validity of exculpatory clauses in other types of contracts.

V. Housing regulations impose a duty upon the landlord to maintain leased premises in safe condition.
VI. As another example, a bailee may limit his liability except for gross negligence, willful acts, or fraud.

The CORRECT answer is:
A. II, I, VI, IV, III, V
B. I, III, IV, V, VI, II
C. III, V, I, IV, II, VI
D. V, III, IV, I, VI, II

4. I. Since there are only samples in the building, retail or consumer sales are generally eschewed by mart occupants, and in some instances, rigid controls are maintained to limit entrance to the mart only to those persons engaged in retailing. 4.____
II. Since World War I, in many larger cities, there has developed a new type of property, called the mart building.
III. It can, therefore, be used by wholesalers and jobbers for the display of sample merchandise.
IV. This type of building is most frequently a multi-storied, finished interior property which is a cross between a retail arcade and a loft building.
V. This limitation enables the mart occupants to ship the orders from another location after the retailer or dealer makes his selection from the samples.

The CORRECT answer is:
A. II, IV, III, I, V
B. IV, III, V, I, II
C. I, III, II, IV, V
D. I, IV, II, III, V

5. I. In general, staff-line friction reduces the distinctive contribution of staff personnel. 5.____
II. The conflicts, however, introduce an uncontrolled element into the managerial system.
III. On the other hand, the natural resistance of the line to staff innovations probably usefully restrains over-eager efforts to apply untested procedures on a large scale.
IV. Under such conditions, it is difficult to know when valuable ideas are being sacrificed.
V. The relatively weak position of staff, requiring accommodation to the line, tends to restrict their ability to engage in free, experimental innovation.

The CORRECT answer is:
A. IV, II, III, I, V
B. I, V, III, II, IV
C. V, III, I, II, IV
D. II, I, IV, V, III

## KEY (CORRECT ANSWERS)

1. A
2. D
3. D
4. A
5. B

# TEST 3

DIRECTIONS: Questions 1 through 4 consist of six sentences which can be arranged in a logical sequence. For each question, select the choice which places the numbered sentences in the MOST logical sequent. *PRINT THE LETTER OF THE CORRECT ANSWER IN THE SPACE AT THE RIGHT.*

1. I. The burden of proof as to each issue is determined before trial and remains upon the same party throughout the trial. 1.____
   II. The jury is at liberty to believe one witness' testimony as against a number of contradictory witnesses.
   III. In a civil case, the party bearing the burden of proof is required to prove his contention by a fair preponderance of the evidence.
   IV. However, it must be noted that a fair preponderance of evidence does not necessarily mean a greater number of witnesses.
   V. The burden of proof is the burden which rests upon one of the parties to an action to persuade the trier of the facts, generally the jury, that a proposition he asserts is true.
   VI. If the evidence is equally balanced, or if it leaves the jury in such doubt as to be unable to decide the controversy either way, judgment must be given against the party upon whom the burden of proof rests.

   The CORRECT answer is:
   A. III, II, V, IV, I, VI
   B. I, II, VI, V, III, IV
   C. III, IV, V, I, II, VI
   D. V, I, III, VI, IV, II

2. I. If a parent is without assets and is unemployed, he cannot be convicted of the crime of non-support of a child. 2.____
   II. The term "sufficient ability" has been held to mean sufficient financial ability.
   III. It does not matter if his unemployment is by choice or unavoidable circumstances.
   IV. If he fails to take any steps at all, he may be liable to prosecution for endangering the welfare of a child.
   V. Under the penal law, a parent is responsible for the support of his minor child only if the parent is "of sufficient ability."
   VI. An indigent parent may meet his obligation by borrowing money or by seeking aid under the provisions of the Social Welfare Law.

   The CORRECT answer is:
   A. VI, I, V, III, II, IV
   B. I, III, V, II, IV, VI
   C. V, II, I, III, VI, IV
   D. I, VI, IV, V, II, III

3. I. Consider, for example, the case of a rabble rouser who urges a group of twenty people to go out and break the windows of a nearby factory. 3.____
   II. Therefore, the law fills the indicated gap with the crime of inciting to riot.
   III. A person is considered guilty of inciting to riot when he urges ten or more persons to engage in tumultuous and violent conduct of a kind likely to create public alarm.
   IV. However, if he has not obtained the cooperation of at least four people, he cannot be charged with unlawful assembly.

V. The charge of inciting to riot was added to the law to cover types of conduct which cannot be classified as either the crime of "riot" or the crime of "unlawful assembly."
VI. If he acquires the acquiescence of at least four of them, he is guilty of unlawful assembly even if the project does not materialize.

The CORRECT answer is:
A. III, V, I, VI, IV, II
B. V, I, IV, VI, II, III
C. III, IV, I, V, II, VI
D. V, I, IV, VI, III, II

4. I. If, however, the rebuttal evidence presents an issue of credibility, it is for the jury to determine whether the presumption has, in fact, been destroyed. 4.____
II. Once sufficient evidence to the contrary is introduced, the presumption disappears from the trial.
III. The effect of a presumption is to place the burden upon the adversary to come forward with evidence to rebut the presumption.
IV. When a presumption is overcome and ceases to exist in the case, the fact or facts which gave rise to the presumption still remain.
V. Whether a presumption has been overcome is ordinarily a question for the court.
VI. Such information may furnish a basis for a logical inference.

The CORRECT answer is:
A. IV, VI, II, V, I, III
B. III, II, V, I, IV, VI
C. V, III, VI, IV, II, I
D. V, IV, I, II, VI, III

# KEY (CORRECT ANSWERS)

1. D
2. C
3. A
4. B

# PREPARING WRITTEN MATERIAL

# EXAMINATION SECTION

# TEST 1

Questions 1-15.

DIRECTIONS: For each of Questions 1 through 15, select from the options given below the MOST applicable choice, and mark your answer accordingly.

A. The sentence is correct.
B. The sentence contains a spelling error only.
C. The sentence contains an English grammar error only.
D. The sentence contains both a spelling error and an English grammar error.

1. He is a very dependible person whom we expect will be an asset to this division. 1.____

2. An investigator often finds it necessary to be very diplomatic when conducting an interview. 2.____

3. Accurate detail is especially important if court action results from an investigation. 3.____

4. The report was signed by him and I since we conducted the investigation jointly. 4.____

5. Upon receipt of the complaint, an inquiry was begun. 5.____

6. An employee has to organize his time so that he can handle his workload efficiantly. 6.____

7. It was not apparent that anyone was living at the address given by the client. 7.____

8. According to regulations, there is to be at least three attempts made to locate the client. 8.____

9. Neither the inmate nor the correction officer was willing to sign a formal statement. 9.____

10. It is our opinion that one of the persons interviewed were lying. 10.____

11. We interviewed both clients and departmental personel in the course of this investigation. 11.____

12. It is concievable that further research might produce additional evidence. 12.____

13. There are too many occurences of this nature to ignore. 13.____

14. We cannot accede to the candidate's request. 14.____

15. The submission of overdue reports is the reason that there was a delay in completion of this investigation. 15.____

Questions 16-25.

DIRECTIONS: Each of Questions 16 through 25 may be classified under one of the following four categories:

A. Faulty because of incorrect grammar or sentence structure.
B. Faulty because of incorrect punctuation.
C. Faulty because of incorrect spelling.
D. Correct

Examine each sentence carefully to determine under which of the above four options it is best classified. Then, in the space at the right, write the letter preceding the option which is the BEST of the four suggested above. Each incorrect sentence contains but one type of error. Consider a sentence to be correct if it contains none of the types of errors mentioned, even though there may be other correct ways of expressing the same thought.

16. Although the department's supply of scratch pads and stationary have diminished considerably, the allotment for our division has not been reduced. 16.____

17. You have not told us whom you wish to designate as your secretary. 17.____

18. Upon reading the minutes of the last meeting, the new proposal was taken up for consideration. 18.____

19. Before beginning the discussion, we locked the door as a precautionery measure. 19.____

20. The supervisor remarked, "Only those clerks, who perform routine work, are permitted to take a rest period." 20.____

21. Not only will this duplicating machine make accurate copies, but it will also produce a quantity of work equal to fifteen transcribing typists. 21.____

22. "Mr. Jones," said the supervisor, "we regret our inability to grant you an extention of your leave of absence. 22.____

23. Although the employees find the work monotonous and fatigueing, they rarely complain. 23.____

24. We completed the tabulation of the receipts on time despite the fact that Miss Smith our fastest operator was absent for over a week. 24.____

25. The reaction of the employees who attended the meeting, as well as the reaction of those who did not attend, indicates clearly that the schedule is satisfactory to everyone concerned. 25.____

## KEY (CORRECT ANSWERS)

| | | | |
|---|---|---|---|
| 1. | D | 11. | B |
| 2. | A | 12. | B |
| 3. | A | 13. | B |
| 4. | C | 14. | A |
| 5. | A | 15. | C |
| 6. | B | 16. | A |
| 7. | B | 17. | D |
| 8. | C | 18. | A |
| 9. | A | 19. | C |
| 10. | C | 20. | B |

| | |
|---|---|
| 21. | A |
| 22. | C |
| 23. | C |
| 24. | B |
| 25. | D |

# TEST 2

Questions 1-15.

DIRECTIONS: Questions 1 through 15 consist of two sentences. Some are correct according to ordinary formal English usage. Others are incorrect because they contain errors in English usage, spelling, or punctuation. Consider a sentence correct if it contains no errors in English usage, spelling, or punctuation, even if there may be other ways of writing the sentence correctly. Mark your answer:

A. If only sentence I is correct.
B. If only sentence II is correct.
C. If sentences 1 and II are correct.
D. If neither sentence I nor II is correct.

1. I. The influence of recruitment efficiency upon administrative standards is readily apparant. 1.____
   II. Rapid and accurate thinking are an essential quality of the police officer.

2. I. The administrator of a police department is constantly confronted by the demands of subordinates for increased personnel in their respective units. 2.____
   II. Since a chief executive must work within well-defined fiscal limits, he must weigh the relative importance of various requests.

3. I. The two men whom the police arrested for a parking violation were wanted for robbery in three states. 3.____
   II. Strong executive control from the top to the bottom of the enterprise is one of the basic principals of police administration.

4. I. When he gave testimony unfavorable to the defendant loyalty seemed to mean very little. 4.____
   II. Having run off the road while passing a car, the patrolman gave the driver a traffic ticket.

5. I. The judge ruled that the defendant's conversation with his doctor was a privileged communication. 5.____
   II. The importance of our training program is widely recognized; however, fiscal difficulties limit the program's effectiveness.

6. I. Despite an increase in patrol coverage, there were less arrests for crimes against property this year. 6.____
   II. The investigators could hardly have expected greater cooperation from the public.

7. I. Neither the patrolman nor the witness could identify the defendant as the driver of the car. 7.____
   II. Each of the officers in the class received their certificates at the completion of the course.

8. I. The new commander made it clear that those kind of procedures would no longer be permitted. 8._____
   II. Giving some weight to performance records is more advisable than making promotions solely on the basis of test scores.

9. I. A deputy sheriff must ascertain whether the debtor, has any property. 9._____
   II. A good deputy sheriff does not cause histerical excitement when he executes a process.

10. I. Having learned that he has been assigned a judgment debtor, the deputy sheriff should call upon him. 10._____
    II. The deputy sheriff may seize and remove property without requiring a bond.

11. I. If legal procedures are not observed, the resulting contract is not enforseable. 11._____
    II. If the directions from the creditor's attorney are not in writing, the deputy sheriff should request a letter of instructions from the attorney.

12. I. The deputy sheriff may confer with the defendant and enter this defendants' place of business. 12._____
    II. A deputy sheriff must ascertain from the creditor's attorney whether the debtor has any property against which he may proceede.

13. I. The sheriff has a right to do whatever is necessary for the purpose of executing the order of the court. 13._____
    II. The written order of the court gives the sheriff general authority and he is governed in his acts by a very simple principal.

14. I. Either the patrolman or his sergeant are always ready to help the public. 14._____
    II. The sergeant asked the patrolman when he would finish the report.

15. I. The injured man could not hardly talk. 15._____
    II. Every officer had ought to had in their reports on time.

Questions 16-26.

DIRECTIONS: For each of the sentences given below, numbered 16 through 25, select from the following choices the MOST correct choice and print your choice in the space at the right. Select as your answer:

A. If the statement contains an unnecessary word or expression
B. If the statement contains a slang term or expression ordinarily not acceptable in government report writing.
C. If the statement contains an old-fashioned word or expression, where a concrete, plain term would be more useful.
D. If the statement contains no major faults.

16. Every one of us should try harder. 16._____

17. Yours of the first instant has been received. 17._____

18. We will have to do a real snow job on him. 18.____
19. I shall contact him next Thursday. 19.____
20. None of us were invited to the meeting with the community. 20.____
21. We got this here job to do. 21.____
22. She could not help but see the mistake in the checkbook. 22.____
23. Don't bug the Director about the report. 23.____
24. I beg to inform you that your letter has been received. 24.____
25. This project is all screwed up. 25.____

# KEY (CORRECT ANSWERS)

1. D
2. C
3. A
4. D
5. B

6. B
7. A
8. D
9. D
10. C

11. B
12. D
13. A
14. D
15. D

16. D
17. C
18. B
19. D
20. D

21. B
22. D
23. B
24. C
25. B

# TEST 3

DIRECTIONS: Questions 1 through 25 are sentences taken from reports. Some are correct according to ordinary English usage. Others are incorrect because they contain errors in English usage, spelling, or punctuation. Consider a sentence correct if it contains no errors in English usage, spelling, or punctuation, even if there may be other ways of writing the sentence correctly. Mark your answer:

A. If only sentence I is correct
B. If only sentence II is correct
C. If sentences I and II are correct
D. If neither sentence I nor II is correct

1. I. The Neighborhood Police Team Commander and Team Patrolmen are encouraged to give to the public the widest possible verbal and written disemination of information regarding the existence and purposes of the program. 1.____
   II. The police must be vitally interelated with every segment of the public they serve.

2. I. If social gambling, prostitution, and other vices are to be prohibited, the law makers should provide the manpower and method for enforcement. 2.____
   II. In addition to checking on possible crime locations such as hallways, roofs yards and other similar locations, Team Patrolmen are encouraged to make known their presence to members of the community.

3. I. The Neighborhood Police Team Commander is authorized to secure, the cooperation of local publications, as well as public and private agencies, to further the goals of the program. 3.____
   II. Recruitment from social minorities is essential to effective police work among minorities and meaningful relations with them.

4. I. The Neighborhood Police Team Commander and his men have the responsibility for providing patrol service within the sector territory on a twenty-four hour basis. 4.____
   II. While the patrolman was walking his beat at midnight he noticed that the clothing stores' door was partly open.

5. I. Authority is granted to the Neighborhood Police Team to device tactics for coping with the crime in the sector. 5.____
   II. Before leaving the scene of the accident, the patrolman drew a map showing the positions of the automobiles and indicated the time of the accident as 10 M. in the morning.

6. I. The Neighborhood Police Team Commander and his men must be kept apprised of conditions effecting their sector. 6.____
   II. Clear, continuous communication with every segment of the public served based on the realization of mutual need and founded on trust and confidence is the basis for effective law enforcement.

7. I. The irony is that the police are blamed for the laws they enforce when they are doing their duty. 7.____
II. The Neighborhood Police Team Commander is authorized to prepare and distribute literature with pertinent information telling the public whom to contact for assistance.

8. I. The day is not far distant when major parts of the entire police compliment will need extensive college training or degrees. 8.____
II. Although driving under the influence of alcohol is a specific charge in making arrests, drunkeness is basically a health and social problem.

9. I. If a deputy sheriff finds that property he has to attach is located on a ship, he should notify his supervisor. 9.____
II. Any contract that tends to interfere with the administration of justice is illegal.

10. I. A mandate or official order of the court to the sheriff or other officer directs it to take into possession property of the judgment debtor. 10.____
II. Tenancies from month-to-month, week-to-week, and sometimes year-to-year are termenable.

11. I. A civil arrest is an arrest pursuant to an order issued by a court in civil litigation. 11.____
II. In a criminal arrest, a defendant is arrested for a crime he is alleged to have committed.

12. I. Having taken a defendant into custody, there is a complete restraint of personal liberty. 12.____
II. Actual force is unnecessary when a deputy sheriff makes an arrest.

13. I. When a husband breaches a separation agreement by failing to supply to the wife the amount of money to be paid to her periodically under the agreement, the same legal steps may be taken to enforce his compliance as in any other breach of contract. 13.____
II. Having obtained the writ of attachment, the plaintiff is then in the advantageous position of selling the very property that has been held for him by the sheriff while he was obtaining a judgment.

14. I. Being locked in his desk, the investigator felt sure that the records would be safe. 14.____
II. The reason why the witness changed his statement was because he had been threatened.

15. I. The investigation had just began then an important witness disappeared. 15.____
II. The check that had been missing was located and returned to its owner, Harry Morgan, a resident of Suffolk County, New York.

16. I. A supervisor will find that the establishment of standard procedures enables his staff to work more efficiently. 16.____
II. An investigator hadn't ought to give any recommendations in his report if he is in doubt.

17. I. Neither the investigator nor his supervisor is ready to interview the witness. 17.____
II. Interviewing has been and always will be an important asset in investigation.

18. I. One of the investigator's reports has been forwarded to the wrong person. 18.____
II. The investigator stated that he was not familiar with those kind of cases.

19. I. Approaching the victim of the assault, two large bruises were noticed by me. 19.____
II. The prisoner was arrested for assault, resisting arrest, and use of a deadly weapon.

20. I. A copy of the orders, which had been prepared by the captain, was given to each patrolman. 20.____
II. It's always necessary to inform an arrested person of his constitutional rights before asking him any questions.

21. I. To prevent further bleeding, I applied a tourniquet to the wound. 21.____
II. John Rano a senior officer was on duty at the time of the accident.

22. I. Limiting the term "property" to tangible property, in the criminal mischief setting, accords with prior case law holding that only tangible property came within the purview of the offense of malicious mischief. 22.____
II. Thus, a person who intentionally destroys the property of another, but under an honest belief that he has title to such property, cannot be convicted of criminal mischief under the Revised Penal Law.

23. I. Very early in it's history, New York enacted statutes from time to time punishing, either as a felony or as a misdemeanor, malicious injuries to various kinds of property: piers, boos, dams, bridges, etc. 23.____
II. The application of the statute is necessarily restricted to trespassory takings with larcenous intent: namely with intent permanently or virtually permanently to "appropriate" property or "deprive" the owner of its use.

24. I. Since the former Penal Law did not define the instruments of forgery in a general fashion, its crime of forgery was held to be narrower than the common law offense in this respect and to embrace only those instruments explicitly specified in the substantive provisions. 24.____
II. After entering the barn through an open door for the purpose of stealing, it was closed by the defendants.

25. I. The use of fire or explosives to destroy tangible property is proscribed by the criminal mischief provisions of the Revised Penal Law. 25.____
II. The defendant's taking of a taxicab for the immediate purpose of affecting his escape did not constitute grand larceny.

## KEY (CORRECT ANSWERS)

1. D
2. D
3. B
4. A
5. D

6. D
7. C
8. D
9. C
10. D

11. C
12. B
13. C
14. D
15. B

16. A
17. C
18. A
19. B
20. C

21. A
22. C
23. B
24. A
25. A

# TEST 4

Questions 1-4.

DIRECTIONS: Each of the two sentences in Questions 1 through 4 may be correct or may contain errors in punctuation, capitalization, or grammar. Mark your answer:

A. If there is an error only in sentence I
B. If there is an error only in sentence II
C. If there is an error in both sentences I and II
D. If both sentences are correct.

1. I. It is very annoying to have a pencil sharpener, which is not in working order. 1.____
   II. Patrolman Blake checked the door of Joe's Restaurant and found that the lock has been jammed.

2. I. When you are studying a good textbook is important. 2.____
   II. He said he would divide the money equally between you and me.

3. I. Since he went on the city council a year ago, one of his primary concerns has been safety in the streets. 3.____
   II. After waiting in the doorway for about 15 minutes, a black sedan appeared.

Questions 4-8.

DIRECTIONS: Each of the sentences in Questions 4 through 8 may be classified under one of the following four categories:

A. Faulty because of incorrect grammar
B. Faulty because of incorrect punctuation
C. Faulty because of incorrect capitalization or incorrect spelling
D. Correct

Examine each sentence carefully to determine under which of the above four options it is BEST classified. Then, in the space at the right, print the capitalized letter preceding the option which is the BEST of the four suggested above. Each faulty sentence contains but one type of error. Consider a sentence to be correct if it contains none of the types of errors mentioned, even though there may be other correct ways of expressing the same thought.

4. They told both he and I that the prisoner had escaped. 4.____

5. Any superior officer, who, disregards the just complaints of his subordinates, is remiss in the performance of his duty. 5.____

6. Only those members of the national organization who resided in the Middle west attended the conference in Chicago. 6.____

7. We told him to give the investigation assignment to whoever was available. 7.____

8. Please do not disappoint and embarass us by not appearing in court. 8.____

Questions 9-13

DIRECTIONS: Each of Questions 9 through 13 consists of three sentences lettered A, B, and C. In each of these questions, one of the sentences may contain an error in grammar, sentence structure, or punctuation, or all three sentences may be correct. If one of the sentence in a question contains an error in grammar, sentence structure, or punctuation, print in the space at the right the capital letter preceding the sentence which contains the error. If all three sentences are correct, print the letter D.

9. A. Mr. Smith appears to be less competent than I in performing these duties. 9.____
   B. The supervisor spoke to the employee, who had made the error, but did not reprimand him.
   C. When he found the book lying on the table, he immediately notified the owner.

10. A. Being locked in the desk, we were certain that the papers would not be taken. 10.____
    B. It wasn't I who dictated the telegram; I believe it was Eleanor.
    C. You should interview whoever comes to the office today.

11. A. The clerk was instructed to set the machine on the table before summoning the manager. 11.____
    B. He said that he was not familiar with those kind of activities.
    C. A box of pencils, in addition to erasers and blotters, was included in the shipment of supplies.

12. A. The supervisor remarked, "Assigning an employee to the proper type of work is not always easy." 12.____
    B. The employer found that each of the applicants were qualified to perform the duties of the position.
    C. Any competent student is permitted to take this course if he obtains the consent of the instructor.

13. A. The prize was awarded to the employee whom the judges believed to be most deserving. 13.____
    B. Since the instructor believes his book is the better of the two, he is recommending it for use in the school.
    C. It was obvious to the employees that the completion of the task by the scheduled date would require their working overtime.

Questions 14-20.

DIRECTIONS: In answering Questions 14 through 20, choose the sentence which is BEST from the point of view of English usage suitable for a business report.

14. A. The client's receiving of public assistance checks at two different addresses were disclosed by the investigation. 14.____
B. The investigation disclosed that the client was receiving public assistance checks at two different addresses.
C. The client was found out by the investigation to be receiving public assistance checks at two different addresses.
D. The client has been receiving public assistance checks at two different addresses, disclosed the investigation.

15. A. The investigation of complaints are usually handled by this unit, which deals with internal security problems in the department. 15.____
B. This unit deals with internal security problems in the department usually investigating complaints.
C. Investigating complaints is this unit's job, being that it handles internal security problems in the department.
D. This unit deals with internal security problems in the department and usually investigates complaints.

16. A. The delay in completing this investigation was caused by difficulty in obtaining the required documents from the candidate. 16.____
B. Because of difficulty in obtaining the required documents from the candidate is the reason that there was a delay in completing this investigation.
C. Having had difficulty in obtaining the required documents from the candidate, there was a delay in completing this investigation.
D. Difficulty in obtaining the required documents from the candidate had the affect of delaying the completion of this investigation.

17. A. This report, together with documents supporting our recommendation, are being submitted for your approval. 17.____
B. Documents supporting our recommendation is being submitted with the report for your approval.
C. This report, together with documents supporting our recommendation, is being submitted for your approval.
D. The report and documents supporting our recommendation is being submitted for your approval.

18. A. The chairman himself, rather than his aides, has reviewed the report. 18.____
B. The chairman himself, rather than his aides, have reviewed the report.
C. The chairmen, not the aide, has reviewed the report.
D. The aide, not the chairmen, have reviewed the report.

19. A. Various proposals were submitted but the decision is not been made. 19.____
    B. Various proposals has been submitted but the decision has not been made.
    C. Various proposals were submitted but the decision is not been made.
    D. Various proposals have been submitted but the decision has not been made.

20. A. Everyone were rewarded for his successful attempt. 20.____
    B. They were successful in their attempts and each of them was rewarded.
    C. Each of them are rewarded for their successful attempts.
    D. The reward for their successful attempts were made to each of them.

21. The following is a paragraph from a request for departmental recognition consisting of five numbered sentences submitted to a Captain for review. These sentences may or may not have errors in spelling, grammar, and punctuation: 21.____
(1) The officers observed the subject Mills surreptitiously remove a wallet from the woman's handbag and entered his automobile. (2) As they approached Mills, he looked in their direction and drove away. (3) The officers pursued in their car. (4) Mills executed a series of complicated manuvers to evade the pursuing officers. (5) At the corner of Broome and Elizabeth Streets, Mills stopped the car, got out, raised his hands and surrendered to the officers.
Which one of the following BEST classifies the above with regard to spelling, grammar, and punctuation?
    A. 1, 2, and 3 are correct, but 4 and 5 have errors.
    B. 2, 3, and 5 are correct, but 1 and 4 have errors.
    C. 3, 4, and 5 are correct, but 1 and 2 have errors.
    D. 1, 2, 3, and 5 are correct, but 4 has errors.

22. The one of the following sentences which is grammatically PREFERABLE to the others is: 22.____
    A. Our engineers will go over your blueprints so that you may have no problems in construction.
    B. For a long time he had been arguing that we, not he, are to blame for the confusion.
    C. I worked on his automobile for two hours and still cannot find out what is wrong with it.
    D. Accustomed to all kinds of hardships, fatigue seldom bothers veteran policemen.

23. The MOST accurate of the following sentences is: 23.____
    A. The commissioner, as well as his deputy and various bureau heads, were present.
    B. A new organization of employers and employees have been formed.
    C. One or the other of these men have been selected.
    D. The number of pages in the book is enough to discourage a reader.

24. The MOST accurate of the following sentences is: 24.____
    A. Between you and me, I think he is the better man.
    B. He was believed to be me.
    C. Is it us that you wish to see?
    D. The winners are him and her.

## KEY (CORRECT ANSWERS)

| | | | |
|---|---|---|---|
| 1. | C | 11. | B |
| 2. | A | 12. | B |
| 3. | C | 13. | D |
| 4. | A | 14. | B |
| 5. | B | 15. | D |
| 6. | C | 16. | A |
| 7. | D | 17. | C |
| 8. | C | 18. | A |
| 9. | B | 19. | D |
| 10. | A | 20. | B |

| | |
|---|---|
| 21. | B |
| 22. | A |
| 23. | D |
| 24. | A |

www.ingramcontent.com/pod-product-compliance
Lightning Source LLC
Chambersburg PA
CBHW082205300426
44117CB00016B/2682
* 9 7 8 1 7 9 9 3 0 8 3 7 9 *